Give Your Heart to Jesus
& Seek the Face of God

by: Paris E. Moore

WESTBOW
P R E S S®
A DIVISION OF THOMAS NELSON
& ZONDERVAN

WestBow Press books may be ordered through booksellers or by contacting:

WestBow Press
A Division of Thomas Nelson & Zondervan
1663 Liberty Drive
Bloomington, IN 47403
www.westbowpress.com
1 (866) 928-1240

ISBN: 978-1-9736-2132-4 (sc)
ISBN: 978-1-9736-2133-1 (e)

Library of Congress Control Number: 2018902896

Print information available on the last page.

WestBow Press rev. date: 06/27/2018

Train up a child in the way he should go: and when he is old, he will not depart from it.

—Proverbs 22:6 (NKJV)

When I was a child, I spake as a child, I understood as a child, I thought as a child: but when I became a man, I put away childish things.

—1 Corinthians 13:11 (NKJV)

Dear friends, do not believe every spirit, but test the spirits to see whether they are from God, because many false prophets have gone out into the world. This is how you can recognize the Spirit of God: Every spirit that acknowledges that Jesus Christ has come in the flesh is from God, but every spirit that does not acknowledge Jesus is not from God. This is the spirit of the antichrist, which you have heard is coming and even now is already in the world. You, dear children, are from God and have overcome them, because the one who is in you is greater than the one who is in the world. They are from the world and therefore speak from the viewpoint of the world, and the world listens to them. We are from God, and whoever knows God listens to us; but whoever is not from God does not listen to us. This is how we recognize the Spirit[a] of truth and the spirit of falsehood.

1 John 4:1-6 (NIV)

CONTENTS

PREFACE

"Prepare and strengthen yourself for what is coming" (Jeremiah 1:17 NIV). Practice is over! Don't Compromise! Don't be afraid. Be informed, engaged, stabilized and directed by God.

I believe we are living at the end of the end of days right now. Jesus could come back at any second. It's time to answer the same question Elijah posed in 1 Kings 18:21 (NKJV). Elijah went before the people and asked, "How long will you waver between two opinions? If the LORD is God, follow Him; but if Baal is god, follow him." But the people said nothing. In other words, the people refused to take personal responsibility for actions because they didn't want to be accountable. How would you respond to Elijah? Is the Lord of Abraham, Jacob, and Isaac your God as well? Or are you wavering between opinions, ideas, philosophies, religions, or practices?

On a scale of zero to ten, how important is your relationship with God? You are the only one who can answer this question. You are the only one who will pay the consequences as a result. A time is coming very soon when the mandate will go forth for everyone to receive a mark on their right hand or forehead. Anyone wanting to purchase health care, food, clothing, housing, among other things will need the mark. No mark, no food! Revelation 13:16 and 19:20 (NKJV) are very clear. Revelation tells us anyone who receives the mark is worshipping the beast and the image.

Proverbs 3:5-6 NKJV tells us what to do in the face of adversity. We are supposed to trust in the Lord with all of our heart and lean not on our own understanding. In all of our ways, we are to acknowledge Him, and He shall direct our paths. It goes on to say, "Be not wise in our own eyes: fear (respect and reverence), the LORD and depart from (disconnect and walk away from) evil. Why? Because it shall be health to our navel and marrow to our bones." If you declare with your mouth, "Jesus is Lord," and believe in your heart God raised Him from the dead, you will be saved (Romans 10:9-10 NKJV). God will take care of us. When we do that, God will hear from heaven, forgive our sins, and heal our land (2 Chronicles 7:14 NKJV). Daniel is just one of many examples in the Bible who teaches us how to stand for God no matter how bad things get. Daniel had to make a choice then, and we have to make a choice now. The good news is that we don't have to be perfect. We just have to be sincere about what we say we believe.

While we can know the signs of the times, we don't know the hour or the day Jesus will come back for us, His church. Mark 13:32 (NKJV) is very clear about that. With that said, we must begin to operate deliberately and on purpose just like the five wise virgins mentioned in the parable in Matthew 5. We must prepare to practice hearing the voice of God and obey immediately. Second Timothy 3 (NKJV) tells us perilous times are coming, and God wants us, His church, to be ready. But how do we prepare? We study the Word of God, the Bible (2 Timothy 2:15 NKJV). We need to know and understand the purpose and application of repentance, salvation, fasting, prayer, rest, and more. What is God saying to you today?

This Bible study, workbook, and journal invites the reader to do the following:

Give your whole *heart* to Jesus and *seek* the *face* of God. *Trust* in the Lord with all your *heart, seek* ye *first* the kingdom of God, and *live* a *life pleasing* to Him.

Grow in your knowledge of the Bible in a way that gives you a clearer understanding of *who* you are, *who* the Most High of the Bible has called you to be, *what* God wants you to *do* about it, and *how* to cooperate *with Him* on *His* terms, not yours. Make a deliberate, personal decision about the direction you want to take in your life.

Invest in your uniquely personal relationship with the God of the Bible. Discover how *He* responds to you. Then learn to search the Bible consistently to be sure the *information* received is in keeping with *what God's* Word says about it (1 John 4 NKJV). *We must practice hearing and recognizing His still, small voice.*

> ➤ **How do we give, grow, and invest in our relationship with God?**

Enter into a right relationship with God. Romans 10:9–10 (NIV) says, "*If* you shall confess with your mouth the Lord Jesus and shall believe in your heart God has raised Him from the dead, you shall be saved. With the *heart* man believes unto righteousness and with the *mouth* confession is made unto salvation."

Maintain your relationship with God. Second Chronicles 7:14 (NIV) says, "*If* My people, who are called by My Name, shall humble themselves, pray, seek My face and turn from their wicked ways; then will I hear from Heaven, I will forgive their sin and will heal their land."

Reinforce your Relationship with God. Second Timothy 2:15 (NIV) says, "*Study* to show yourself approved unto God, a worker who needs not be ashamed, rightly dividing the Word of truth."

Understand your relationship with God. Matthew 6:6 (KJV) says, "But you, when you pray, enter into your closet and when you have shut your door, *pray* to your Father in secret and your Father Who sees in secret, shall reward you openly."

Be confident in your relationship with God. First Peter 2:9 (KJV) says, "But you *are* a chosen generation, a royal priesthood, a holy nation, a peculiar people; you should show forth the praises of Him Who has called you out of darkness into His marvelous light." (Peculiar means not usual or normal.)

> ➤ **What separates us from God?**

Sin means "to miss the mark." It does not remove salvation.

Transgression refers to presumptuous sin. It means "to choose to *intentionally* disobey, willfully trespassing.

Iniquity is more deeply rooted. Iniquity refers to a *premeditated* choice, continuing without repentance.

> ➤ **What brings us back into a right relationship with God?**

Repentance is a feeling of responsibility for wrongdoing.

Repent means "to cause to feel regret or contrition; to feel sorrow, regret or contrition for; to change one's mind, turn from sin and try again, not just sorry for getting caught." God is calling for *His* people to stand firm and to be like Jesus. We must be ambassadors for Christ (2 Corinthians 5:20 NKJV) while we are still here on earth. Hebrews 13:14-15 (NIV) makes our mission clear. It reminds us this world is not our home. We are to look forward to that which is to come. With God's help and in the name of His dear Son, Jesus allows us to continually offer our sacrifice of praise by proclaiming His glorious name and increasing in the knowledge of Christ daily.

The idea of this book came to me as I began to identify and research the root causes and reasons for the hardships I experienced. Some were obvious and easy to resolve, while others were not. Simply put, I did not have a close enough walk with God. It is important to walk close with God so that when the time comes to comply with the mandate for all people to get a mark on the right hand or forehead, we will be able to be like Daniel and trust God no matter how the events are presented to us. (See the case of Daniel 6:2-28 NKJV.) Yesterday it was Daniel. Today it could be you.

According to Ecclesiastes 1:9 (NKJV), there is nothing new under the sun. If that is true, I should be able to find my situation in the Bible study and compare my lifestyle choices with what the Word of God has to say. Then I can decide to either *stop* what I'm doing, *start* doing something *new*, or *make* the *changes* necessary to support my stand. I prayed for wisdom, understanding, direction, and application as often as I remembered. I wrote down the time, date, and description of what happened (see "Prayer, Prophecy, Dream, and Vision Journal") and compared them with biblical principles.

I needed specific answers to specific questions from knowledgeable people. I would have gladly taken courses, but I could not find one that encompassed everything I needed in one field of study. Instead I asked questions of God and people, read a lot, made notes, and applied the new information as I learned it. I was willing to learn from my mistakes, and I made changes as often as I needed to and accepted trial and error as my tools of choice.

During this time, my husband and I lost his source of income and our home in the 2008 housing crash. There were lots of changes taking place in my job too. In addition to that, we had been driving junk cars. When I couldn't make arrangements for a ride, I had to drive. I named our car the "Prayer Mobile" because I prayed for the safety of others and us before we got in it. I would thank God when we parked. God protected us every single time. To God be the glory!

By the time I got home, my nerves were on edge, and my anxiety was high. The thought of putting my family back in the Prayer Mobile was more than I could handle. Fear and anxiety became my constant companions. Plus, I was diagnosed with high blood pressure. I was prescribed medication to manage it, and eventually, I was prescribed a second medication. I hated the fact there was a problem with my blood pressure. I was already physically active, and my body type was naturally small, so losing weight to control my blood pressure was not an option.

I also developed chronic nose bleeds that seemed to show up out of nowhere. I needed help to figure out why they started and how to stop them. Sometimes after a nose bleed, I would be fatigued for a day or so. I worked with children, so this was not a good mix. I loved working with the children, but the high blood pressure, nose bleeds, family struggles, and financial problems were taking a toll.

I knew I was fighting depression. I didn't like the possibility of taking even more medication. We always had something to eat, but it was not always substantial. My husband and I were doing what we could to make ends meet. We worked our jobs, were active members in our church, helped others, and prayed to God for help. I was an ordained minister who tithed until I felt I could not do it anymore.

We were trying to find our way out of that nightmare as soon as possible. While God did not cause this situation, He was using it to provide insight so that we could grow and teach others about His goodness in ways totally beyond our ability to understand. I didn't realize I was writing a book. I'm not sure when it switched from research notes to a workbook and journal.

As you go through this process, remember we serve a forgiving God. He loves us and does not want us to be misled. The Bible tells us we will have hardships (Matthew 5:11–12 NKJV). By dealing with our own heart condition and developing a strong and intimate relationship with God, our faith will increase, our trust in God will be reinforced, and we will be able to stand strong because of God, who is working in us (Hebrews 11:1 KJV).

When I looked for my situation in the Bible (see "Bible Case Study"), I discovered the woman in 2 Kings 4:26 (NKJV). She was experiencing a hardship much greater than mine, and when someone asked her how she was doing, she replied, "All is well." She was confident in God's ability to come through for her. I decided to follow her example. When people asked me how I was doing, I said, "I am well." I didn't say that because I was well but because I was aspiring to become confident in God's ability to come through for me.

ACKNOWLEDGMENTS

I acknowledge Yahweh, the One and only true God, the God of Abraham, Isaac and Jacob in the Holy Bible.

I acknowledge Jesus (Yeshua), the Son of God (Yahweh) Who was crucified, anointed and buried, but Yahweh raised Him from the dead and He appeared to witnesses before He ascended into Heaven, where He is seated at the right hand of the Father (Yahweh).

I acknowledge when the fullness of time is complete, Yeshua will return with the clouds and every eye will see Him, even those who pierced Him, and all tribes of the Earth will wail on account of him. Even so, come LORD Jesus. Amen.

TESTIMONY: DIVINE CONNECTIONS

Divine connections were set up by Yahweh, the One and only true God in the Name of His dear Son, Jesus (Yeshua). Thank you, God (Yahweh) for the people who are called by your name. Amen.

I thank God for my husband Larry who put up with my piles of papers and books, for proofreading and encouraging me to stick with it even during my weakest times. And for our children and grandchildren and family. They inspire me.

When God put this book on my heart, I didn't have a clue of what to do so I prayed for divine wisdom, connections, finances and application.

Nancy Sorrell, (a former newspaper editor) a sister in Christ began encouraging me and doing a little editing in the beginning. When I had done the best, I could with the information she shared, I prayed again and asked God to tell me what to do next. Almost immediately I felt impressed to call my friend *Colleen Tronson*, (another sister in Christ). I told her I was praying for an editor for my book who was a doer of the Word and knew God personally. Colleen suggested I give *Susan Mowen* a call; so, I did. We talked, and *Susan* accepted the task. I left my manuscript with her and walked away confident (for this project) *Susan* was God's best. Turns out Susan is a book editor, biblical scholar and a missionary too. Wow, what a blessing!

True to form as I inquired of the Lord and was taking my next best steps, when I printed out the last few pages of the manuscript. My thought was what should I do next? And how much will it cost? Once again, I felt impressed. Impressed to go to a place I hadn't been yet. The impression on my spirit was to go to Staples. "Staples?" I said out loud. It felt a little strange, but I did it anyway and asked for one copy of the manuscript. That's when I met *Suzanna Smith*, who began asking me a lot of questions. Questions I didn't know the answers to yet. Her leading questions were great learning tools because researching and learning the answers is what brought this book and book cover to you.

One day I attempted to describe to Suzanna the picture God had given me in a dream. I even showed her the attempt of a picture I drew. That's when Suzanna shared the vision for her ministry. A ministry (she thought) she had not yet begun but little did she know at that very moment God was using her to impact and encourage me to keep moving on. I would learn later Suzanna was in her last month of becoming a graphic artist.

And there is more. As I was going through the writing, editing and design process, I enlisted the help of some of God's veterans. Thank you to: Dr. Jill Jackson, pastor, evangelist and teacher. Dale Johnson, a follower of Christ and a student of the Bible. John Snowburg, a map maker and Sister Junie Maloney, an international missionary, for their comments, insights, knowledge and wisdom.

God bless Jeannie Ramsure and Colleen Tronson for helping, crying, laughing and dancing with me during the good, the bad and the ugly. For loving God the way you all do
And just plain being you.
I thank God, He loves you and I do too.

OVERVIEW

I hope that chapters one through seven will help the reader to know and understand exactly what God has called them to do; where He has called them to serve; how to differentiate the voice of God from an imposter every time. We are the body of Christ and we need each other on the front lines of faith.

Read about the problems, personalities, situations, and choices the individuals of The Bible had to contended with. Learn how they dealt with obstacles that kept them from moving forward with their relationship with God.

Identify things that may keep you from moving forward in your relationship with God. Discover what the Bible says about the things you have identified.

Evaluate relationship(s) connections and their consequences; Discover how thoughts and feelings (inward conditions) can activate behaviors (outward manifestations). Decide, on purpose, if these conditions and manifestations are taking you in the direction you want to go. Understand what, Systems-of-Delivery are and how you are impacted by them.

Consider and appreciate: the human internal organ systems, thought and memory process, need to rest and what they have to do with how you choose to maintain your relationship with God.

Design a plan of action, create a support system that includes relationship accountability that can help you reach your goal.

God spoke to the people in, The Holy Bible, and He is still speaking to us today. Yahweh, Our Lord, does not want us to be afraid. He wants us to be informed, equipped and able to operate in this world as agents of change. We are the people who are called by His Name, and who come in the name of His Dear Son, Jesus, The Christ.

If we can't believe God will help us with the mundane (i.e., things taking place in this world rather than heaven), how will we believe Him for the miraculous (i.e., things that are excellent in a way that suggests a marvelous event outside of normal causation).

INTRODUCTION

Dear Reader, I was in prayer at 4:22 a.m. on July 6, 2013. I felt impressed to write these words that came into my heart. Read the words that follow and judge for yourself.

"I am giving you a heavy mantle to tell people to seek Me while I may be found. Don't worry about where to start just **start somewhere**. Perilous times are coming and I Jesus am the only way out" (2 Timothy 3 KJV, emphasis added). As the Lord says, "You need complete and total trust in Me. I will tell My people things the world can't know unless I (God) reveal it to them. I don't need a GPS. system, the medical profession, the global market, the food and drug administration, or a sovereign nation because all of these things already belong to Me. I am God!

"My Word reveals who I am and what I have done (Ecclesiastes 1:9 NIV). There is nothing new under the sun. I will continue to do that which I have done. Seek Me in this midnight hour while I may still be found (Isaiah 55:6 NIV). Tell the people to give their hearts to Jesus and seek the face of God. Read the Bible, and the Holy Spirit will bring you into all truth concerning My plans and the plans of the adversary for your life. Choose ye this day, which you will serve, and then go that way. The judgment seat is an appointed time for everyone (2 Corinthians 5:10 NIV).

"Tell them I love them. I made them for My glory to walk and fellowship with Me. They are the delight of My heart when they praise Me, when they give to others and help one another in My name (Deuteronomy 15:11 KJV). Come to Me all those who are heavy-laden, and I will give you rest (Matthew 11:28 NKJV). If My people who are called by My name will humble themselves and turn from their wicked ways (disobedience to God in any way is wicked), then I will hear from heaven. I will be their God, and they will be My people (2 Chronicles 7:14 NKJV). Now hide My Word in your hearts as fast as you can and walk with Me so I can be your real, legal, and righteous protector, God the Father, the almighty and highest living God (Psalm 119:11 NKJV).

"God is not willing that any should perish (2 Peter 3:9 KJV). We are in the very last days. Come to Me now! When I call you out, I will make the way possible for you to go. This message is the same for everybody (Acts 2:17 NKJV). The time has come when the things in this life will do you no good unless they are directed by Me. Nothing you have is sacred, and you can't bring it here. So use it there to bless and be blessed (Mark 8:36 NKJV). Be willing to open your mind to Me. I want to do so much for you, but you limit Me. Your thinking is too small. I am God. I will do wondrous and miraculous acts because I love you and I know the plans I have for you to do well, but I can have no partnership with a double-minded man (individual) (James 1:8 NKJV). How will you know My voice unless you know Me wholly and become single-minded about who I really am in your life? (Proverbs 3:5–6 NIV; Ephesians 29:11 NIV; James 1:8 NIV; Matthew 6:33 NIV).

"I am God, the Creator and owner of all things (Colossians 1:16 NIV). Now is the time to pray for individual souls to be saved and hearts and minds turned to Me (Romans 13:11 NIV). The worldly position of a person is not important, only the position of your heart toward Me (Revelation 3:15–16 NIV; 1 John 1:9 NIV). Pray for everyone to turn to Me while I may still be found (Isaiah 55:6 NIV; Mark 8:36 NIV; Revelation 3:15–16 NIV)."

As a disciple of the gospel, I believe that the Bible is the inspired Word of God, that Jesus is the Son of God in the flesh, that only through faith in Jesus can anyone become a child of God, and the child of God must obey the Word of God to please Him.

Romans 3:23 (NIV) says, "For all have sinned and fall short of the glory of God."

Romans 6:23 (NIV) says, "For the wages of sin is death; but the gift of God is eternal life through Jesus Christ our Lord."

Acts 3:19 (NIV) says, "Repent then, turn to God, so your sins may be wiped out, that times of refreshing may come to you from the Lord" (meaning restoring your spirit).

Don't wait until things are all figured out in your life. Now would be the perfect time to invite Jesus into your heart (if you haven't already done so) using whatever words express your desire to know Him personally. May God bless and keep you.

If you have not already done so, please make your relationship with God your number-one priority.

Repent, for no person will be justified (Romans 3:23 NIV).

"If you confess with your mouth Jesus is Lord and believe in your heart God raised Him from the dead, you will be saved" (Romans 10:9–10 NLT). Talk to God just like you would talk to a friend. Talking to God is called prayer.

Study the Bible so you can understand the meaning of the Word of God. Ask God for wisdom and understanding as you read. Memorize a scripture or two to start.

Fast (abstain from food while continuing to drink fluids, keeping in mind your medical and dietary needs) with wisdom. Make time with God the center of your attention. If you are on a medical plan or are taking medication be sure to consult with your medical care provider before making your decision. Ask them to help you create a plan that is right for you. You might want to start with the Danial Fast or abstain from screens (tv, movies, video games, youtube, etc.)

Plan the type of fast you will be doing. Know the objective of the fast. Decide on the duration. Plan your Bible study and prayer time. Don't put pressure on yourself. Just do the best you can with what you have. God honors a sincere heart. One purpose of fasting is to help us experience the impact of the power of God's ability to keep us we go through this process. Start small and grow from there. Decide on the plan and keep it doable.

Pray! Prayer is a two-way conversation with God. There is a time to tell Him what is on your mind, a time to talk to Him about the needs of others, and a time to listen for His response.

Go as God leads you. Live according to the Word of God. Do what the Bible says a Christlike person should do and don't do what the Bible says a Christlike person should not do. In other words, ask yourself, "What would Jesus do?" And then do that.

Give your heart to Jesus and seek the face of God. God is still speaking and His power is still flowing today. (See 1 Kings 19:11–13 KJV.)

Our first example of God speaking is found in Genesis 1:3 (NKJV). "And God said, 'Let there be light;' and there was light." Genesis 1:3–31 (NKJV) is an account of what God said and what happened as a result. There are parables in the Bible to help us develop our understanding, but most of what is written is a report about real events. There is documented historical, archaeological, and geographical evidence the people, places, and events recorded in the Bible really did exist. This makes the Bible a creditable account.

For this reason, we will do case studies of situations found in the Bible. A case study is a published report about a person, group, or situation studied over time. It's also a situation in real life that we can examine to learn about something. The published reports we will be using come from the Bible.

God is looking for a submissive praying people who enact His Word. The questions that must be answered are as follows:

- Do you perceive God as a source of power that may or may not work on your behalf?
- Is He a source of power that's able to deliver you from and utterly destroy the works of the devil?

Consider the case of the man in Mark 5 who would (by today's standards) probably be diagnosed with some type of schizophrenia or bipolar disorder. When you study this account, you will find Jesus caused this man to be delivered. He was able to sit still, remain fully dressed, and operate in his right mind. John 14:12 (KJV) tells us that we will not only do the same things Jesus did but that we (the body of Christ) will do even more.

To accomplish these things, we must live a life consecrated and pleasing to God. The only way to do that is to study the Bible with the help of the Holy Spirit, who exalts Jesus and also convicts, regenerates, lives in, seals, guides, and comforts us. He enables us to understand and apply what is taught in the Bible and encourages us to worship God.

Chapter 1

Bible Study

The purpose of our case-by-case Bible study is threefold. *First*, take the issue you are wrestling with and find it in the Bible. *Second*, identify the root cause and learn how it was dealt with. *Third*, bring the information forward to see how it applies today.

Ecclesiastes 1:9 (NKJV) says, "What has been, will be again, what has been done, will be done again; there is nothing new under the Sun." Ephesians 6:12 (NIV) says, "We wrestle not against flesh and blood, but against principalities, powers, rulers of the darkness of this world, against spiritual wickedness in high places." It's time to do your homework.

The Bible is as true today as it was for the people in the Old and New Testaments. What is it you struggle to remove from or add to your life? It's time to understand it, make a decision about it, and let God guide you according to His plan and purpose for your life. We are running out of time.

While there are parables in the Bible to help our understanding, most of what is written is taken from real-life biblical events. There is documented proof that the people, places, and events of the Bible were real. This makes the Bible a credible account. *God said it, and it is so!*

Let's begin our study. Pick at least two (or more) of the fifteen Bible cases provided. Read the full accounts in the Bible before you begin the discussion. These Bible cases by no means make up an exhaustive list. There are so many wonderful options from which to choose.

Part 1

This process is meant to prove the issues we deal with today are virtually the same as the ones the people dealt with in the Bible—that is, with two exceptions, specifically modern-day amenities and calendar dates. There are people in the Bible who did irresponsible and horrible things. God forgave them when they repented, but they still had to deal with the consequences of the choices they made.

Case #1: This boy's name is Joseph. He was the biological son of a wealthy man who favored him over his ten half-brothers. Joseph was not taken seriously by his family. He spoke without weighing the potential consequences and was perceived as a tattletale. When he was seventeen he was sold into slavery by his brothers. They told his father he was dead. **Joseph experienced:** favoritism, hatred, betrayal, and slavery. Even in that he continued to keep his word to God even though it was not a popular thing to do. Joseph always kept God first and did his best work. The people who kept him as a slave respected him, his abilities and his God. Joseph was promoted to leadership positions often. **Scripture reference:** Genesis 37:1–36 NASB) **Can you identify with this character or situation in any way?**

Case #2: This man's name is Moses. He was targeted for death at birth by the government, adopted and raised by royalty. The birth of Moses would mark the beginning of God's plan to free His people from four hundred years of Egyptian slavery. God had a plan for Moses and He has a plan for you. Once Moses understood the plan God had for his life he decided to do what God told him to do regardless of the consequences he (Moses) would have to endure. As a result Moses and the people witnessed and benifited by: The miracle of the pillar of cloud and fire, the parting of the Yam Suph (Red Sea or Sea of Reeds), God's victory over the Egyptian army, the sweetening of the bitter water at Marah, the miracle of the quails, the miracle of the manna, bread from heaven, the miracle of the life-giving water from the rock, and the defeat of the Amalekites at Rephidim. **Moses experienced:** a speech impediment, was insecure, self-consciuos, and had major spiritual and political responsibilities. **Scripture reference:** Exodus 1-10 (NASB) **Can you identify with this character or situation in any way?**

Case #3: This lady's name is Princess Michal. She found herself in the kind of family feud many women face. This family feud determined the future of a nation. Princess Michal was used as a pawn, first by her father and then by her husband. She was betrayed, neglected and taken advantage of by the men who were supposed to love and protect her. **Princess Michal experienced:** trust issues, depression and outrage. She was angry, barren and involuntarily isolated from others. She despised her husband and didn't seek God. She disappears from the list of names in the family. **Scripture reference:** 1 Samuel 18:20-30; 19:13 (NASB) **Can you identify with this character or situation in any way?**

Case #4: Name: King David wanted another man's wife. Her name was Bathsheba. He sent for and had sex with her. When Bahsheba became pregnant King David had Uriah (her husband, a loyal dedicated soldier and citizen) moved to the front lines so that he would be killed. David's baby by Bahsheba died. Many of David's soldiers and family members lost trust and respect for him. David repented to God and changed his ways. Nathan, a prophet of God, told David that God had forgiven him. David's wife became pregnant again and gave birth to a healthy son named Solomon who became the next king. **David experienced:** Being a murderer, extreme selfishness, greed, and being a backslider. David chose to listen to Nathan's rebuke. Nathan told David he was wrong and David took personal responsibility for his choices but had to live with the consequences of his actions for the rest of his life. **Scripture reference**: 2 Samuel 11:1–26; 12:1–31 (NASB) **Can you identify with this character or situation in any way?**

Case #5: The widow at Zarephath had no food and resources. Her son could have been forced into slavery because she could not pay off the family debt. Her husband was a man of God but left no inheritance for them when he died. She and her only child were hungry. During this time the people were experiencing severe drought and famine. She was preparing to die along with her son. Elijah the prophet (the proven man of God) told her exactly what to do. She made up her mind to trust his words. As a result the widow had enough money to pay all the debt and feed her family until the drought was over. **The widow experienced**: Fear, anger, confusion, betrayal, depression, starvation and restoration. **Scripture reference**: 2 Kings 4:1–7 (NASB) **Can you identify with this character or situation in any way?**

Case #6: This is Queen Esther, her real name was Hadassah but she could not let her captors know. She was an orphan raised by her uncle Mordecai. Esther became a leader when she was a teenager and during adverse times. A man was planning to kill the Jews and destroy their culture. Esther found out about the plan and sent a message to tell her uncle to gather together all the Jews in Susa to fast and pray with her. She said, "Do not eat or drink for three days, night or day. I and my attendants will fast as well. When this is done, I will go to the king, even though it is against the law and if I die, I die." Esther and her people put God first. God vindicated and saved the people. **Esther experienced**: Fear, disappointment, depression, anxiousness, entrapment and total dependence on God. **Scripture reference**: Esther (NASB) **Can you identify with this character or situation in any way?**

Case #7: Danial had coworkers who were jealous of him and made a plan to make him look bad, lose his job, and crush his future. They wanted to cause his boss who *respected* him to kill him. Danial lived what he believed and was thrown into a pit of hungry lions (for real) because of it. Daniel would have been at least ninety and possibly more than hundred years old at the time. His boss the king wanted him to bow down and worship him. Danial respectfully declined. Daniel continued to pray only to his God even though he knew he might have to face the lion's den. Daniel continued to kneel down upon his knees three times a day, pray, and gave thanks to his God just as he did every day before for the law was passed. Daniel was put in the lion's den but was protected through it all. **Danial experienced**: betrayal, personal eminent danger and faith in his personal relationship with his God. **Scripture Reference**: Daniel 6:1–28 (NASB) **Can you identify with this character or situation in any way?**

Case #8 Jesus got in a boat and his disciples followed him. They were caught in a violent storm, frightening, potentially life-threatening storm and they were afraid. Instead of rebuking (releasing the power of God themselves) the storm. They called on Jesus to do it. **They experienced**: intense fear, lack of faith evidence that the power of Jesus is real. **Scripture reference**: Matthew 8:23–27 (NASB) and Luke 8:22–25 (NASB) They experienced: intense fear. **Can you identify with this character or situation in any way?**

Case #9: Jesus Christ is the Savior (Yeshua). This is the greatest love story ever lived. He was betrayed, brutalized, and left for dead. The story includes His birth, teaching, miracles, betrayal, crucifixion, resurrection, ascension, and return. **Jesus experienced**: Betrayal, unspeakable hatred, pain, agony and punishment, spiritual, mental and emotional abuse. Jesus didn't use His power to save Himself from the cross. Jesus did what God wanted Him to do during the good and bad times. **Scripture references:** Matthew 1:28-25; 9:35; 26:36-46 (NASB); Mark 15:33-34 (NASB); Luke 2:1-20; 22:39-46; 23:32-43 (NASB); Acts 1:1-12 (NASB) **Can you identify with this character or situation in any way?**

Case #10: Herod and Herodias had a relationship built on the sins of lust, greed, and selfishness. Herod threw a huge birthday party for himself. He invited the high officials and important people in the region. Most of them came. Herod made a promise he regretted immediately, but he kept it because he didn't want to look bad in front of his friends. God allows us to make our own choices. God did not stop them. **Herod experienced**: drunkenness, manipulation, anger, resentment, revenge, pride, and being a murderer. **Scripture reference:** Matthew 14:1-12 (NASB); Mark 6:14-29 (NASB) **Can you identify with this character or situation in any way?**

Case #11: A homeless man who lives at a tumb was crying and cuts himself day and night. He was a social outcast, menace to society. He publicly asked Jesus for help. As a result the man was found at Jesus's feet. The demons were gone, and he was in his right mind. **He experienced**: compulsive cutting, physical infirmities, sickness or diseases, rage, super-human strength, mental health problems, mental and physical torment and isolation. He was a danger to himself and others. **Scripture reference:** Mark 5:1-20 (NASB); Luke 8:27 (NASB) **Can you identify with this character or situation in any way?**

Case #12: A woman with an issue of blood hemorrhaged for twelve years. She was a social outcast, and she was financially bankrupt. She was considered unclean, and everything she touched was considered unclean too. She had a medical condition that probably began in puberty. She could not work. She spent all her money trying to find a cure. Her condition continued to deteriorate. She was doubled over in pain and could not stand up straight. She heard about Jesus and believed He could help her. She did whatever she had to do to get close to Jesus and touch His cloak because she knew Jesus could heal her. She pushed through the crowd and touched Him and Immediately, her bleeding stopped, and she felt free from her suffering. **She experienced**: problems getting daily needs met, consistent fatigue, weaknes, fear, disappointment, depression, anxiety, hopelessness, and bleeding. **Scripture reference:** Mark 5:21-34 (NASB); Luke 8:40-48 (NASB) **Can you identify with this character or situation in any way?**

Case #13: This boy thrown in the fire and water. He had no control over his own body. His father was looking for help for his son because he (the father) could not help him. The son suffered terribly. He had convulsions that caused him to fall into fire and water involuntarily. He foamed at the mouth gnashed his teeth. Consequently, his teeth became ridged. He was a social outcast. He and his family endured much physical, emotional, and mental suffering since childhood, and he was (sometimes) mute.

His father brought him to Jesus because the disciples couldn't help them. The father never gave up. Jesus made the unclean spirit leave, healed the child, and gave him back to his father. **They experienced**: pain, suffering, embarrassment, and searching for hope. **Scripture reference:** Mark 9:14-29 (NASB) **Can you identify with this character or situation in any way?**

Case #14: The Samaritan woman at the well. She had been married five times and was living (in sin) with a man who wasn't her husband. She decided to talk with Jesus. She admitted her sin, repented, and gave her testimony to others. She knew she didn't know Him, but He knew everything about her and was able to make a difference in her life. She experienced prejudice, injustice, being a social outcast and had a bad reputation. **Scripture reference:** John 4:1-44 (NASB) **Can you identify with this character or situation in any way?**

Case #15: The crippled beggar was totally dependent on others. He was carried to and from his accustomed begging place daily. He had congenital disease, was physically and financially dependent on family, friends and community. He asked Peter and John for alms (money or food given to poor people) but got physically healed instead. This man was willing to receive what the man of God had to offer. The request was made of God in the name of *Jesus*. This is an example of a direct link between earth and heaven. Peter is on earth, and Jesus is in heaven. This connection released the power of God through the man of God to heal the beggar. This is *faith* in *action*. The apostle Peter took him (the crippled man) by the right hand and lifted him up. Immediately, his feet and ankle bones received strength. The man stood, walked, and entered the temple with them, leaping and praising God. **He experienced:** weakness, humility, embarrassment, tenacity, joy and healing. **Scripture reference:** Acts 3 (NASB) **Can you identify with this character or situation in any way?**

Part 2

In part 1, we looked at the published report, the Bible. In part 2, find a story in the Bible that reflects a person, place, thing, or event you have dealt with in the past, you are dealing with now, or you must deal with in the future. Fill in the information here.

Case #1

1. What are you focusing on? Give the name of the person, place, thing, or event.

2. Write a short summary of your situation.

3. Find a Bible case like your situation to study.

4. Write the scripture reference, verses, and Bible version.

5. Describe similarities between the case study and your situation.

6. Give the specific person, decision, and event which brought things into agreement with God in the Bible case study. Describe the person, decision, or event you feel would bring things in your life into agreement with God.

7. What was the tangible evidence God intervened in the Bible case study? What evidence are you praying for God to bring about in your situation?

8. List the things you have in common with the person, decision, or event you studied.

9. Discuss commonalities, possible resolution options, personal growth possibilities, and how to keep God involved on a regular basis.

Case #2

1. What are you focusing on? Give the name of the person, place, thing, or event.

2. Write a short summary of your situation.

3. Find a Bible case like your situation to study.

4. Write the scripture reference, verses, and Bible version.

5. Describe similarities between the case study and your situation.

6. Give the specific person, decision, and event that brought things into agreement with God in the Bible case study. Describe the person, decision, or event you feel would bring things in your life into agreement with God.

7. What was the tangible evidence God intervened in the Bible case study? What evidence are you praying for God to bring about in your situation?

8. List the things you have in common with the person, decision, or event you studied.

9. Discuss commonalities, possible resolution options, personal growth possibilities, and how to keep God involved on a regular basis.

In part 1, we looked at the published report, the Bible. In part 2, you picked Bible cases that you felt had something in common with your situation. In part 3, pick a specific situation in your life that needs to be resolved and fill in the information here.

Keep your personal information private. If you don't feel comfortable filling in the blanks, then interact with this information in a way that best suits your needs. Remember, the only person you can change is you. Do it in a way that keeps you safe.

Case #1

1. What do you want God to do?

2. What were some similarities between your situation and the Bible case study in step two?

3. List changes (you need to make) to bring your situation into agreement with the will of God.

4. What is the exact event or situation you are praying to resolve?

5. Discuss possible resolutions, options, personal growth possibilities, and how to keep God involved on a regular basis as you mature in Christ.

Case #2

1. What do you want God to do?

2. What were some similarities between your situation and the Bible case study in step two?

3. List changes (you need to make) to bring your situation into agreement with the will of God.

4. What is the exact event or situation you are praying to resolve?

5. Discuss possible resolutions, options, personal growth possibilities, and how to keep God involved on a regular basis as you mature in Christ.

Chapter 2

Personal Inventory

From the last chapter, you will find that the issues of yesterday are the same as the issues we wrestle with today. Now it's time to go even deeper. Be intentional. Discover how to become the consistently dedicated and consecrated Christian you want to be. Plan how to protect your decision and create a plan to turn your lifestyle choices into your reality.

Ecclesiastes 1:9 (NASB) is clear in reporting what has been and will be again. There is nothing new under the sun. The Bible case studies have shown we are dealing with the same issues today the people in the Bible did. When the people of the Bible aligned their thoughts, choices, and actions with the way God told them to live, things began to change for them. Some changes happened immediately, and some took a while. In each case, it was better with God than without Him.

Continue to identify the things you wrestle with and see what God has to say about them, decide what you should do about it. Plan a strategy and work your plan. *Are you as close to God as you want to be, or is it your desire to get even closer? The choice is yours, and so are the consequence(s).* You are the *only one* who can strengthen your walk with God. He created you. He loves you, and He wants to be in your life.

Part 1: Identify things that may keep you from moving forward in your relationship with God.

A. List three things you find yourself worried, frustrated, anxious, or afraid about most often. This could include bills, health, relationships, jobs, careers, employment, housing, education, lack of education, family, and/or the future.

B. List three emotions you find yourself dealing with most. Give the connection between the emotion and the cause. For example, you could write, "I am afraid to spend money because I never have enough, and I don't know when I will have more." *Fear* is the emotion. The possibility of not having enough or knowing when money will come is doubt. *Doubt* is the connection.

Other emotions could be love, hate, forgiveness, un-forgiveness, resentment, bitterness, and/or hopelessness.

C. List three words that describe your physical health most often or include any diagnosis obtained from a health care professional.

D. List specific persons, places, things, or events that may cause you to stress. For example, you could list a person whose opinion you value, a place you need to visit but find unpleasant, or something you must do but are nervous about.

E. List three of the ways you respond to stress. For example, you may think about swearing, throwing things, working out, taking frustrations and anger out on others, counting to ten, keeping things bottled up inside, drinking, gambling, fighting, breathing exercises, blaming yourself, and/or being apologetic all the time.

Part 2

God is willing to love, forgive, protect, provide, and send warnings, directives, and corrections to us. Start with one of your answers from part 1 in studying the Bible.

For example, my first choice was to learn more about the fear I listed as one of the emotions I wrestled with most. I chose to study the life of Daniel because I think he had to have been afraid at some point. But how did he not give in to it? How can I learn to trust God even during my fear and sorrow? My scripture reference was Daniel 6:1–28 (NASB). I learned Daniel never had to get ready to trust God because of the lifestyle choices he made. Daniel never had to get ready because he lived ready. No matter how good or bad things got for him, he never stopped doing the things that connected him to God, whom he loved. As evidence, God gave him information and protected him as he lived his life.

A. Please give an example.
1. What did your Bible case study reveal about the emotions and connections you find yourself dealing with most?

2. Write the scripture reference and Bible version.

3. Write a summary of what you read and how it applies to you.

B.
1. What did your Bible case study reveal about the state of your health or diagnosis?

2. Find an example in the Bible and give the scripture reference which speaks best to your situation.

3. Write a summary of what you read and how it applies to you.

C.
    1. What did your case study reveal about allowing people, places, things or events to take your peace?

    2. Find an example in the Bible and give the scripture reference and Bible version which speaks best to your situation.

    3. Write a summary of what you read and how it applies to you.

D.
    1. What did your case study reveal about the way you respond to stress?

    2. Find an example in the Bible and give the scripture reference which speaks best to your situation.

    3. Write a summary of what you read and how it applies to you.

Part 3
Bring your discoveries forward and plan your application.

A.
    1. What do you know now that you didn't know before your Bible study about worry, anxiety, or fear?

    2. Explain how this information will help you in the future?

B
    1. What does the Bible say about sickness and disease?

2. Explain how this information will help you in the future?

C.

1. What does the Bible say about allowing people, places, things, or events to take away your peace?

2. Has this information or perspective changed anything for you?

3. Explain.

D.

1. What does the Bible say about stress?

2. Has this information or perspective changed anything for you?

3. Explain.

Part 4

Now is the time to decide where to start your deeper walk with Jesus.

1. Pick a person, place, thing, or event.

2. Decide what you will need to do to start, stop, or make changes successfully.

3. Pick a time frame (hours, weeks, months, years) as a check-in point.

4. Identify and set well-defined boundaries and expectations for you and your accountability support person(s). Plan how you will maintain your accountability and how you will evaluate your progress. *Remember to reevaluate when necessary.* It's better to do well in small steps than to run full speed ahead. If something is not working well, make some changes and keep on moving, but never give up. When you fall, get back up. Learn the lesson, leave the trash behind, and respect the journey.

A. List three things you need to change or stop completely. Explain.

B. List three things you could do to support the three things you listed previously.

C. List three benefits that will happen because of the choices you have made.

D. List three things you need to start doing. Explain.

E. List three things already working well. Explain how you know.

Planning Suggestions
- giving
- fasting
- accountability
- setting well-defined boundaries for relationships
- studying
- resting
- praying
- sharing the gospel
- reevaluations
- other

Chapter 3

Evaluate Relationship Connections and Consequences

Make a decision that will take you in the direction you want to go with a clear understanding of the consequence(s). Are you trying to get closer to God, or are you as close to God as you desire to be? How can we expect something supernatural from God while we willingly stay connected to Satan? This is not a tug-of-war. Clearly, the power in the name of Jesus is dominant. God will always allow you to walk through your lifestyle choice. Everything you do, think, and say reveals something about the deity you are connecting with at the time.

Example #1: In writing this book, God is helping me remember so that I can help you. As I have come to understand the dangers of occultism practices mentioned in Deuteronomy 18:9–12 (NASB) and the importance of getting rid of the paraphernalia connecting me to them, I repent as often as the need arises. I also thank God for His mercy and forgiveness. This particular memory would have devastated me except for the power of God. I know now God is able to deliver everyone from bondage. One evening we were playing with a Ouija board. We were having lots of fun. The middle piece was moving very fast around the board. Someone said, "Let's call Jessie James and see what happens." So, we did. After a few minutes, a large grayish plume of smoke showed up in the room. We were dumbfounded. After a few seconds, a young man walked into the room and the smoke seemed to dissipate into him. We all laughed a scared, nervous laugh. We quickly put the board away and never played it again. Sadly, the damage had already been done.

I thank God for the wisdom found in the pages of the Bible and in the power of the name of Jesus. Everything you need to know about how to fight this battle is in the Word of God. If you need help, *ask Jesus to help you, and He will!* It was wrong to think I could play with occult toys and not be impacted by them. In this example, I willingly owned and interacted with paraphernalia and events connected with the god (Satan) of this world.

Example #2: Years ago, I attended a prayer meeting at the YMCA in north Minneapolis. There were six or seven people at prayer that night. During prayer I began to feel overwhelmed like I should get my stuff and go. I was confused about the emotion because I was excited about being there and I wanted to stay. How could I be experiencing both of those emotions at the same level and time? Some of the people were sitting and some were pacing the floor as they prayed. I could hear a voice outside of myself saying, "Go! This is stupid. You are stupid for being here." I could feel a dark and heavy presence speaking mainly into my right ear. While this was going on, I was still trying to pray, and at the same time, I tried to think of a way of telling somebody about this without sounding crazy.

I had this happen to me before, but I never acknowledged it. I looked around to see if anyone else seemed to hear this voice. As I was trying to understand what was happening to me. Pastor Winston was praying in the spirit and walking toward me. He stopped directly in front of me and began talking directly to that presence. It felt to me like Pastor Winston and that presence were having an argument and I was standing in the middle of it! I was so amazed because Pastor spoke directly to what the presence (which was a demonic spirit as I later learned) was saying to me. It was like the pastor could see it and hear exactly what it was saying to me. I had never experienced anything like that. It seemed crazy and wonderful at the same time. The pastor rebuked that thing, and after a few minutes, it stopped talking. I ended up crying tears that had been suppressed for years. That spirit was gone. God made a way through that prayer meeting for me to get the confirmation I needed.

What I was experiencing was real, and the true man of God was able to do something about it. I thank God for that man and his beautiful wife. They were both praying that night. I felt the feeling of fear leave and the feeling of peace come over me. My thoughts became calm and peaceful. Never did I think I would ever tell this story. People need to understand God. His love and power are real. In this example I was engaged with the people and the event that connected with Jesus, the Son of God, through the power of God.

First Peter 5:8–9 (NASB) says, "Be of sober spirit, be on the alert. Your adversary, the devil, prowls about like a roaring lion, seeking someone to devour. But resist him, firm in your faith, knowing the same experiences of suffering are being accomplished by your brethren who are in the world."

Know that Satan attempts to devour us by setting up systems to deliver his brand of deception in ways that seem harmless. Proverbs 14:12–13 (NASB) says, "There is a way of life which looks harmless enough; look again, it leads straight to hell." Sure, those people appear to be having a good time, but all that laughter will end in heartbreak. When I was dabbling in occult practices, I didn't know that was what I was doing. I thought I was doing it "just for fun." I was a good person and would never hurt anyone on purpose. This seemed harmless to me, but it was an abomination to God, whom I was trying to serve.

Deuteronomy 18:9–14 (NASB) says, when you enter the land the LORD your God is giving you, do not learn to imitate the detestable ways of the nations there. Let no one be found among you who sacrifices their son or daughter in the fire, who practices divination or sorcery, interprets omens, engages in witchcraft, or casts spells, who is a medium or separatist or who consults the dead. Anyone who does these things is detestable to the LORD; because of these same detestable practices, God will drive out those nations before you. You must be blameless before the LORD your God. The nations you will dispossess listen to those who practice sorcery or divination. But as for you, the LORD your God has not permitted you to do so.

This was my wake-up-call. I wasn't looking for one, but it came anyway.

For the sake of our discussion I am describing a *system-of-delivery* as a way of doing things or a method of thinking made of many interdependent or related parts. Each part is connected to a philosophy or thought process driving the choices we make, all of which connect us to a specific person, place, or thing. God, the Creator of all things, has a system-of-delivery, and Satan, the Father of Lies, has a system-of-delivery. But whose system(s) are you connecting to, and why? We either align our lives with God or not. There is no in-between.

In other words, *pick a side!* I know God can use anything and everything to bring us into the knowledge of Christ. When you sincerely want to know about God, He will make a way to draw you to Himself.

To be connected to God's system-of-delivery or way of doing things, you must do the following. The things listed here are a good place to start. The first two are musts.

Accept Jesus as your Lord and Savior: "If you declare with your mouth, "Jesus is LORD," and believe in your heart God raised Him from the dead, you will be saved. For it is with your heart you believe and are justified, it is with your mouth you profess your faith and are saved" (Romans 10:9-10 NIV).

Repent: "Repent, then and turn to God, so your sins may be wiped out, that times of refreshing may come from the Lord" (Acts 3:19 NIV).

Study the Bible: "All scripture is given by inspiration of God and is profitable for doctrine, reproof, correction, and instruction in righteousness: That the man of God may be perfect, thoroughly furnished unto all good works" (2 Timothy 3:16–17 KJV).

Live by faith: "But without faith, it is impossible to please Him: for he who comes to God must believe He is and He is a rewarder of them who diligently seek Him" (Hebrews 11:6 NKJV). Living by faith is being supernaturally aware of who God is and what He wants you to do without knowing or understanding all the details or outcomes. God, leads by the Spirit away from flesh. When we walk with God, He leads us by and into kingdom principles. The closer we walk with God, the quicker the things of this world will lose their appeal. When you walk with God, this world is no longer a contender for your heart. When you are connected with God's system-of-delivery, you don't have to be afraid because God knows what to do. If you get into position, you can *hear* the still, small voice of God telling you what to do because *nothing* can surprise, overcome, or overtake Him.

Forgive: If you forgive other people when they sin against you, your heavenly Father will also forgive you, but if you do not forgive others their sins, your Father will not forgive your sins (Matthew 6:14–15 NIV).

To be connected to Satan's system-of-delivery or way of doing things, you must do the following:
Sin: Sin means "to miss the mark." So whoever knows the right thing to do and fails to do it, for him it is sin (James 4:17 ESV).

Transgress: You may violate a command or law. You may go beyond a boundary or limit of what God says to do or not to do.

Commit iniquity: This is more deeply rooted. *Iniquity* means "premeditated choice, continuing without repentance." David's sin with Bathsheba, which led to the killing of her husband, Uriah, was iniquity (2 Samuel 11:3–4; 12:9 NIV). Micah 2:1 (NIV) says, "Woe to those who plan iniquity, to those who plot evil on their beds! At morning's light they carry it out because it is in their power to do it." In David's psalm of repentance, he cries out to God, saying, "Wash away all my iniquity and cleanse me from my sin" Psalm 51:2 NIV).

A. God
Example 1. The Bible.
Every Christian should read and study the Bible daily.

Example 2. Prophecy/Word of Knowledge
God said to me, "Tell My people there is always going to be a fight if you want to see Me clearly. Satan is always going to have billboards, bands playing, people turning flips and acrobats between you and Me. I am calling on you (the church) to press toward the mark of the high calling I have for you to live and not die. *Turn off all noise and seek the face of God.*

B. Satan
Example 1. Entertainment/Movies
I went to see the *Hobbit: The Desolation of Smaug* (Jackson, 2013). I was surprised this movie brought the *leviathan* (written about in Job 40 and 41) to the big screen. These scriptures tell about the Behemoth, a huge dinosaur-like animal that is called Leviathan. God is telling Job that He (God) created it, and He goes on to describe it in detail. God tells Job this creature is without fear and nothing on earth is its equal. Therefore, man cannot control or kill it. Only God can handle it. In the movie, this huge dinosaur-like animal was terrorizing a city. As folklore would have it, there was only one man who could use a special javelin to kill the creature, but he would have to throw it right into its heart. That's what happened, and that is how the creature died. This movie was full of fairies, magic powers, sorcery, and demonic entities. In my opinion,

this is just one example of a satanic system-of-delivery delivering satanic messages (thoughts) and dogma through entertainment. My take-away was that you don't need God but that you need magic. That's a lie! The system of delivery was a movie. The message of the movie aimed to say that you can be saved by the ungodly practices that the Bible warns us to completely avoid.

Example 2. Entertainment/Movies that Seem Biblical but Aren't
These mediums are mixed with exciting special effects and some ungodly events. For example, consider *Exodus: Gods and Kings* (Scott, 2014). It starts out confusing and stays that way until the end. During the movie you see the burning bush. Then you see a child who is sitting with goats and talking with the Moses type character. This child is the god figure in the movie. He is doing and saying things counter to the character of the living God.

I am praying for the people who look to these movies to understand biblical things. Please pray for these people so that they will search out the real truth in the Bible for themselves.

There are many systems (methods, or ways) that deliver either the true word of God or lies from the enemy's (Satan's) camp. I have listed a few.

God's System-of-Delivery (This is by no means an exhaustive list)
The Gospel– Is a message of salvation and hope in the Name of Jesus Christ of Nazareth

Blessing are God's way of providing for His people.

Deliverance in the Bible is the act of God whereby He rescues His people from peril. In the Old Testament, deliverance is focused primarily on God's removal of those in the midst of trouble or danger.[1]

Discernment is given by God through His Holy Spirit. It is received through God's Word and through the insight of a renewed mind. Discerning believers seek to grow in their understanding and knowledge of God's truth.[2]

Dreams are a series of thoughts, images, and sensations occurring in a person's mind during sleep.[3]

Faith is strong belief or trust in someone or something; belief in the existence of God.[4]

Fasting is going without something (mainly food) for a period of time in order to cleanse (and ultimately strengthen) the body, soul, mind, or all of the above (my definition).

---

[1] (https://gotquestions.org/deliverance.html)
[2] (http://biblehub.com/topical/dbt/8227.htm)
[3] (https://en.oxforddictionaries.com/definition/us/dream)
[4] (http://pediaa.com/difference-between-faith-and-belief)

Fellowship is building relationships with like-minded people who also love, cherish, and are devoted to Jesus.[5]

Holy Days are from God. They are M*oade* or M*oadim a* Hebrew word meaning appointed time, a festival)—God's appointed time to teach us to remember things He has done for His people (see Leviticus 23:2).[6]

Prayer is a two-way conversation that consist of talking with and listening to God.[7]

Prophecy is God's intentions voiced through man to confirm God is all-knowing.

Repentance is the action of repenting having sincere regret or remorse and literally turning away from.[8]

Vision is an experience of seeing someone or something in a dream or trance or as a supernatural apparition.[9]

Satan's System-of-Delivery (This is by no means an exhaustive list)

Adultery is having a Voluntary sexual encounter or relationship between a married person and someone other than his or her spouse. *Synonyms* include cheating, infidelity, misconduct, two-timing, unfaithfulness, thought, and porn.[10]

Channeling is a modern name for what the Bible calls mediumship or spiritism. A channeler is a mystic who becomes a channel or receptive agent for intelligent communications coming from the spirit world. What does God say about mediumship? It's in the Bible Leviticus 19:31 (NIV) says, "Do not turn to mediums or seek out spiritists, for you will be defiled by them".[11]

Charm is the chanting or reciting of a magic spell, incantation; the practice or expression believed to have magic power; something worn about the person to ward off evil or ensure good fortune: amulet; a trait that fascinates, allures or delights; compelling attractiveness. A small ornament worn on a bracelet or chain.[12]

Charmer is a person skilled in using supernatural forces, the legendary charmer known as the Pied Piper of Hamelin.[13] Synonyms include conjurer (or conjuror), enchanter, mage (magician),

---

[5] (http://www.whatchristianswanttoknow.com/christian-fellowshi-quotes-22-edifying-quotes)

[6] (http://www.triumphpro.com/holy-days-book.pdf)

[7] (http://www.tellingthetruth.org/hot-topics/prayer/what-is-prayer.aspx)

[8] (http://www.encyclopedia.com/humanities/dictionaries-thesauruses-pictures-and-press-releases/repent)

[9] (https://en.oxforddictionaries.com/definition/vision)

[10] (http://www.merriam-webster.com/dictionary/adultery)

[11] (http://www.bibleinfo.com/en/questions/what-does-god-say-about-channeling-and-mediums)

[12] (http://www.merriam-webster.com/dictionary/charm)

[13] (http://www.merriam-webster.com/thesaurus/charmer)

magian (magi), magus (one magician), necromancer, sorcerer, voodoo, voodooist, witch, wizard. enchantress, hag, hex, sorceress, warlock, occultist, thaumaturge (magician), thaumaturgist, theurgist (Egyptian magician), wonder-worker, medicine man, shaman, shamanist, witch doctor, crystal gazer, diviner, foreseer, fortune-teller, prognosticator, prophesier, prophet, seer, soothsayer, medium, exorciser, andexorcist.[14]

Chaldean is a member of an ancient Semitic people who became dominant in Babylonia; a person versed in the occult arts.[15]

Days of the week (names): The English words for each day bear remnants of Roman tradition, but they have been filtered through centuries of Germanic and Norse mythos. The Germanic people adapted the Roman system by identifying Roman gods with their own deities.

> **Sunday** comes from the Old English Sunnandæg, which is derived from a Germanic interpretation of the Latin *dies solis*, meaning "sun's day." Germanic and Norse mythology personify the sun as a goddess named Sunna or Sól.

> **Monday** likewise comes from Old English Mōnandæg, named after Máni, the Norse personification of the moon (and Sól's brother).

> **Tuesday** comes from Old English "Tīwesdæg," after Tiw or Tyr, a one-handed Norse god of dueling. He is equated with Mars, the Roman war god.

> **Wednesday** is "Wōden's day." Wōden or Odin was the ruler of the Norse gods' realm associated with wisdom, magic, victory, and death. The Romans connected Wōden to Mercury because they were both guides of souls after death. Wednesday comes from Old English Wōdnesdæg.

> **Thursday**, "Thor's day," gets its English name after the hammer-wielding Norse god of thunder, strength, and protection. The Roman god Jupiter was both the king of gods and the god of the sky and thunder. Thursday comes from Old English Þūnresdæg.

> **Friday** is named after the wife of Odin. Some scholars say her name was Frigg. Others say it was Freya. Other scholars say Frigg and Freya were two goddesses. Whatever her name, she was often associated with Venus, the Roman goddess of love, beauty, and fertility. Friday comes from Old English Frīgedæg.

> As for **Saturday**, Germanic and Norse traditions didn't assign any of their idols to this day of the week. They retained the Roman name instead. The English word Saturday comes

---

14 (http://www.merriam-webster.com/thesaurus/charmer)
15 (https://www.google.com/#q=A+member+of+an+ancient+semitic +people+that+became+dominant+in+Babylonia%3B+a+person+versed+in+the+occult+arts)

from the Anglo-Saxon word Sæturnesdæg, which translates to "Saturn's day" (Genesis 2:1–3 NLV; Psalm 16:4 NLV; Deuteronomy 6:14 NLV; Judges 10:13 NLV; Exodus 20:3 NLV).[16]

Divination—The practice of using signs (such as an arrangement to tea leaves or cards) or special powers to predict the future (Samuel 28:3–25 NIV).[17]

Enchanter is a person who uses spells or magic; a sorcerer or wizard (Samuel 28:3–25 NIV).

Entertainment is amusement or diversion provided especially by performers or something diverting or engaging as a public performance (Mark 6:21–29 NIV; Daniel 5:1–31 NIV).[18]

Familiar spirit is from the Latin *familiaris*, meaning "household servant," and it is intended to express the idea that sorcerers had spirits as their servants that were ready to obey their commands. Those attempting to contact the dead, even to this day, usually have some sort of spirit guide who communicates with them. These are familiar spirits (1 Samuel 28:7 NIV; Acts 16:16–18 NIV).[19]

Familial is of or relating to a family; suggesting a family; tending to affect members of the same family (1 Samuel 28:7 NIV; Acts 16:16–18 NIV).[20]

Graven image, the phrase "graven image" comes from the King James Version and is first found in Exodus 20:4 in the second of the Ten Commandments. The Hebrew word translated as "graven image" means "an idol." A graven image is an image carved out of stone, wood, or metal. It could be a statue of a person or animal or a carving in a wall or pole. It is differentiated from a molten image, which is melted metal poured into a cast. Abstract Asherah poles, carved wooden Ba'als covered in gold leaf, and etchings of idols accompanying Egyptian hieroglyphics are all graven images (1 Kings 18:20–40 NIV; Daniel 1:1–2 NIV).[21]

Holidays (tradition)—These are counterfeits *not* given by God. We celebrate them out of tradition and love for God but in ignorance. Holidays are associated with Nimrod. They include Christmas, Lent, Easter, Valentine's Day, Halloween, Thanksgiving (to the sun god), Sunday worship. Constantine changed Saturday Sabbath to Sunday. We may say we are celebrating them unto God, but what days does God call holy? Holidays exalt idols, and holy days exalt God. Which do you suppose came first—holy days or holidays? One is the authentic, and the other is the counterfeit. You be the judge (Deuteronomy 12:29–32 NIV).[22] Where (in the Bible) does God say to honor holidays? See "holy days" under God's system of delivery.

---

[16] (See http://www.livescience.com/45432-days-of-the-week.html.)

[17] (See also http://www.merriam-webster.com/dictionary/divination.)

[18] (See http://www.merriam-webster.com/dictionary/enchanter.)

[19] (See https://gotquestions.org/familiar-spirits.html.)

[20] (See http://www.merriam-webster.com/dictionary/familial.)

[21] (See http://www.gotquestions.org/graven-image.html.)

[22] (See http://www.nazarite.net/evil-holidays.html.)

Horoscope is advice and future predictions based on the date of a person's birth and the positions of the stars and planets (Leviticus 19:31 NIV).[23]

Idolatry is the worship of any image in the form of anything in heaven above or on the earth beneath or the waters below. (Deuteronomy 18:10–11 NIV).[24]

Magic (sometimes spelled magick) is a power that allows people (such as witches and wizards) to do impossible things by saying special words or performing special actions; tricks that seem to be impossible and done by a performer to entertain people; special power, influence, or skill (Isaiah 8:19 NIV).[25]

Necromancy is the practice of talking to the spirits of dead people; the use of magic powers, especially for evil purposes (Leviticus 20:6 NIV).[26]

Scrying is foretelling the future using a crystal ball or other reflective objects or surface. (Deuteronomy 18:10–11 NIV).[27] Note that anything you can watch has the potential to watch you.

Seared consciences is a result of continual, unrepentant sinning. Eventually, sin dulls the sense of moral right or wrong; the unrepentant sinner becomes numb to the warnings of the conscience God has placed within each of us to guide us (1 Timothy 4:2 NIV).[28]

Spell is a spoken word or set of words believed to have magic power. (The witch cast a spell that turned the prince into a toad) (Deuteronomy 18:10–11 NIV).[29]

Spirit guide—See familiar spirit.

Spiritualism is a system of belief or religious practice based on supposed communication with the spirits of the dead, especially through mediums (1 John 4:1 NIV).[30]

Superstition is a belief or way of behaving based on fear of the unknown and faith in magic or luck; a belief certain events or things will bring good or bad luck (Exodus 20:3–4 NIV).[31]

Warlock is a man who has magical powers and practices witchcraft; a sorcerer or wizard (Exodus 7:8–13 NIV).[32]

---

[23] (See http://www.merriam-webster.com/dictionary/horoscope.)
[24] (See http://www.merriam-webster.com/dictionary/idolatry.)
[25] (See http://www.merriam-webster.com/dictionary/magic.)
[26] (See http://www.merriam-webster.com/dictionary/necromancy.)
[27] (See https://en.oxforddictionaries.com/definition/us/scry.)
[28] (See http://www.kingdomcitizens.org/one-womans-perspective/beware-of-a-seared-conscience.)
[29] (See http://www.merriam-webster.com/thesaurus/spell.)
[30] (See https://www.google.com/#q=spiritualism+definition.)
[31] (See http://www.merriam-webster.com/dictionary/superstition.)
[32] (See http://www.merriam-webster.com/dictionary/warlock.)

Witch is a woman who is thought to have magic powers; a person who practices magic as part of a religion (such as Wicca) (1 Samuel 28:7 NIV).[33]

Witchcraft is Magical things done by witches; the use of magical powers obtained especially from evil spirits (Deuteronomy 18:10-11 NIV).[34]

Wizard—A person skilled in magic or one who has magical powers; a sorcerer or magician.[35]

Yoga—An ascetic Hindu discipline involving controlled breathing; prescribed body positions and meditation with the goal of attaining a state of deep spiritual insight and tranquility. A system of stretching and positional exercises derived from this discipline to promote good health, fitness, and control of the mind (idolatry).[36]

Identify and judge your *relationship connections*. Decide to *stop, continue,* or *change* them based on the kingdom with which you want to align yourself and your eternity. Whatever you are connected to has the authority to impact your life as a blessing or a curse. Inventory everything from your motives to your outfits. You must make the choice to allow it or not.

Some options include education (type), entertainment (type), fashion (type), finances, games (name/type), health (diagnosed or other), hobbies, jewelry (type), living spaces (name/room), music (lyrics), objects (charms/status/other), organizations (public/secret), relationships (type), social media (type), and/or words (blessings/curses).

Here is my first example of a relationship connection. I was watching a movie. During the movie actors were saying, "god" followed by the word, "dam". It made me uncomfortable, but I continued to watch anyway. When an actor said it again I decided to stop watching the move. It was hard. I wanted to know how the move was going to end but at the same time I felt it was wrong. I needed to choose to stay in agreement with the context of the movie by continuing to watch it or stand up for the God that I say I respect and disconnect from the event.

The relationship connection between me and the ungodly behavior was entertainment. The type of entertainment was a move. As long as I watched the move knowing that disrespecting the name of God was going to happen I was also disrespecting God because I didn't do anything to stop it. In this example the relationship connection was entertainment. The type of entertainment was a movie. Below are my example answers to the questions.

Question 1: Does the relationship connection you are engaging in bring order, clutter, or *chaos* into your life? **Answer**: I'm not sure, but I will pick chaos.

---

[33] (See http://www.merriam-webster.com/dictionary/witch.)

[34] (See http://www.merriam-webster.com/dictionary/witchcraft.)

[35] (http://www.merriam-webster.com/dictionary/wizard)

[36] (https://ahdictionary.com/word/search.html?q=yogic)

Explanation: I picked chaos because it makes me uncomfortable when I hear the name of Our Lord being disrespected. Sometimes I tell myself it's *just a* movie. It doesn't make sense to listen to someone who is disrespecting God. Especially for entertainment purposes.

Question 2: Would you say this relationship connection supports the way you feel about God? Yes or no. **Answer:** No.

Explanation: I needed to stop dismissing this as *just* entertainment. Exodus 20:7 (NIV) says, "You shall not misuse the Name of the LORD your God, for the LORD will not hold anyone guiltless who misuses His Name."

Question 3: Should you *stop*, continue, or change the impact this relationship connection has on your life? **Answer:** I should stop it.

Explanation: I should stop watching the movie if I hear this disrespect. God takes it seriously, and I should too. Exodus 20:7 says God will hold you accountable.

Question 4: Would you say the impact of the relationship connection you listed confirms you are hot, cold or *lukewarm* toward God? Answer: Lukewarm

Explanation: If I stop, hot. If I don't, lukewarm. I will stop.

Example 2

Relationship Connection: Finances
Type: Debt

Question 1: Does the relationship connection you have entered bring order, clutter, or *chaos* into your life? **Answer:** clutter

Explanation: I can't seem to settle on giving when I have so little to work with.

Question 2: Would you say this relationship connection supports the way you feel about God? Yes or *no*? **Answer:** No

Explanation: It is hard to provide for my family and give. It is also depressing. I want to be able to give without having to worry about it.

Question 3: Should you *stop*, continue, or change the impact this relationship connection has on your life? **Answer:** I need to make a change.

Explanation: I want to be a good provider for my family and a kingdom giver to God.

Question 4: Would you say the impact of this relationship connection confirms you are *hot*, cold, or lukewarm toward God? **Answer:** Lukewarm.
Explanation: I don't always put God first in my giving. I will get help to learn how to put God first in a way that is good for my family and me.

Relationship Connection Worksheet #1

Identify and judge your *relationship connections*. Decide to *stop, continue,* or *change* them based on the kingdom with which you want to align yourself and your eternity. Whatever you are connected to has the authority to impact your life as a blessing or a curse. Inventory everything from your motives to your outfits. You must make the choice to allow it or not.

Some options include education (type), entertainment (type), fashion (type), finances, games (name/type), health (diagnosed or other), hobbies, jewelry (type), living spaces (name/room), music (lyrics), objects (charms/status/other), organizations (public/secret), relationships (type), social media (type), and/or words (blessings/curses).

After you have chosen the first relationship connection, answer the questions and make a decision on purpose to stop it, allow it to continue, or make the changes necessary for God to bless it.

Relationship Connection: _____
Type:_____

Question 1: Does the relationship connection you have entered bring *order, clutter* or *chaos* into your life? **Answer:**
Explanation:

Question 2: Would you say this relationship connection supports the way you feel about God? Yes or no. **Answer:**
Explanation:

Question 3: Should you *stop, continue,* or *change* the impact this relationship connection has on your life? **Answer:**
Explanation:

Question 4: Would you say the impact of this relationship connection confirms you are *hot, cold,* or *lukewarm* toward God? **Answer:**
Explanation:

Do not be yoked together with unbelievers. What do righteousness and wickedness have in common? What fellowship can light have with darkness? What harmony is there between Christ and Belial? What does a believer have in common with an unbeliever? What agreement is there between the temple of God and idols? We are the temple of the living God. As God has said, "I will live with them and walk among them; I will be their God and they will be my people. Therefore, come out from them and be separate," says the Lord. "Touch no unclean thing and I will receive you. I will be a Father to you and you will be my sons and daughters." (2 Corinthians 6:14–18 NIV).

Relationship Connection Worksheet #2

Identify and judge your *relationship connections*. Decide to *stop*, *continue*, or *change* them based on the kingdom with which you want to align yourself and your eternity. Whatever you are connected to has the authority to impact your life as a blessing or a curse. Inventory everything from your motives to your outfits. You must make the choice to allow it or not.

Some options include education (type), entertainment (type), fashion (type), finances, games (name/type), health (diagnosed or other), hobbies, jewelry (type), living spaces (name/room), music (lyrics), objects (charms/status/other), organizations (public/secret), relationships (type), social media (type), and/or words (blessings/curses).

After you have chosen the first relationship connection, answer the questions and make a decision on purpose to stop it, allow it to continue, or make the changes necessary for God to bless it.

Relationship Connection: _____

Type: _____

Question 1: Does the relationship connection you have entered bring *order*, *clutter* or *chaos* into your life? **Answer:**

Explanation:

Question 2: Would you say this relationship connection supports the way you feel about God? Yes or no. **Answer:**

Explanation:

Question 3: Should you *stop*, *continue*, or *change* the impact this relationship connection has on your life? **Answer:**

Explanation:

Question 4: Would you say the impact of this relationship connection confirms you are *hot*, *cold*, or *lukewarm* toward God? **Answer:**
Explanation:

Do not be yoked together with unbelievers. What do righteousness and wickedness have in common? What fellowship can light have with darkness? What harmony is there between Christ and Belial? What does a believer have in common with an unbeliever? What agreement is there between the temple of God and idols? We are the temple of the living God. As God has said, "I will live with them and walk among them; I will be their God and they will be my people. Therefore, come out from them and be separate," says the Lord. "Touch no unclean thing and I will receive you. I will be a Father to you and you will be my sons and daughters." (2 Corinthians 6:14–18 NIV).

Chapter 4

Fearfully and Wonderfully Made by God

Caroline Leaf, author of *Who Switched Off My Brain: Controlling Toxic Thoughts and Emotions*, explains how the thoughts we think automatically trigger our brains to release chemicals that will impact our bodies in a way that is positive or negative. Proverbs 23:7 (KJV) says, "As he thinks in his heart, so is he: 'Eat and drink,' says he to you; but his heart is not with you." Make a decision to stop, continue, or change things keeping you from deepening your relationship with God.

Be sober. First Peter 5:8 (NIV) says, "Be alert and of sober mind. Your enemy, the devil prowls around like a roaring lion looking for someone to devour." He wants to catch you in your weakness so he can influence your thoughts in a way that gives him the ability to steal, kill, and destroy your life.

I was praying and asking God why I was not able to get rid of the high blood pressure. When I settled down, these are the words that came into my spirit. "A double-minded man is unstable in all his ways." God has not given you the spirit of fear but of power, love, and sound mind. "Satan seizes you on the inside and surrounds you on the outside. I AM, is the same yesterday, today and forever" (James 1:8 NIV).

"What I have against you is your approach is most often out of dread." Instead of making a decision, I usually assumed the outcome would be negative and felt great stress as a result. Dread is fear. Your thoughts focus on fear. What did Elisha have to fear when the soldiers kept coming to him on the mountain? See 2 Kings 1:1–18 (NIV). What did Esther have to fear when she went before the king? See Esther 4:1–17 (NIV). What did Daniel have to fear when he was going to be thrown into the lion's den? (Daniel 6:1–28 NIV). What did Jesus have to fear when He laid His life down at the cross? (Acts 2:23–24 NIV).

"Don't dread the coming circumstances. I AM, is the plan" (James 1:8 NIV; 2 Timothy 1:7 NIV; 2 Kings 6:8–22 NIV; Esther 4:15–17 NIV; Daniel 3:16–18 NIV; Acts 5:30 NIV).

This entry from my prayer journal comes from March 12, 2013 at 5:00 a.m.

I was surprised when I went back and studied what I had written to see if it lined up with biblical precepts. It was true. If the believers (some before Christ and therefore not Christians) in the Bible could trust God for their lives, certainly I could too. I thanked God for speaking to me through His Word. As I continue my Bible case studies, personal inventories, and decision making, my ability to trust God grows even deeper.

We are supposed to love the Lord with all our heart, soul, and mind and love others as we love ourselves. As we align our thoughts with the Word of God, the chemicals in our bodies begin to balance, resulting in homeostasis (balanced chemicals in the body). It is the unbalanced chemicals in the body that can lead to unrest, a state of dissatisfaction, disturbance, or disorder. We even make jokes saying, "My chemicals are out of balance." And so often that is the case.

In the same way a fever is a warning something is wrong in our body, sin is a warning indicating something is wrong in our thinking. Sin is proof we are being influenced, totally overwhelmed, or impacted by something that might be unknown to us at the time. Fever and sin cause an outward magnification of an inward condition.

I have had to pray and ask God which of Satan's devices (satanic systems of delivery) are influencing or impacting me and what I needed to do about it. God led me in the very direction I needed to go. If I had not gone through this process, I could not have written this Bible study, workbook, and journal.

"I praise God because we *are* fearfully and wonderfully made; His works are wonderfully made, I know that fully well." Psalm 139:14 (NIV) expresses the incredible nature of our physical bodies. I read on *gotquestions.org*, "The human body is the most complex and unique organism in the world; that complexity and uniqueness speaks volumes about the mind of our Creator. Every aspect of the body, down to the tiniest microscopic cell, reveals it is nothing less than a miracle" (see https://gotquestions.org/fearfully-wonderfully-made.html).

Let's take a closer look at this body. God formed it out of the dust and breathed the breath of life into its nostrils, and it became a living soul (Genesis 2:7 NIV). *The Illustrated Atlas of the Human Body* by Beverly McMillan states, "The body is a collection of 12 organ systems, each organized to perform a particular function." *McMillan* goes on to say,

> The skin or integument is a multi-purpose outer cover, while bones of the skeletal system provide a supportive physical framework. The body's hundreds of skeletal muscles interact with bones to move the body and its parts. It is nourished by a digestive system that brings in and processes food, releasing nutrients to the blood, eliminating indigestible residues.
>
> Systems for blood circulation and respiration move oxygen, nutrients and other vital supplies to the trillions of body cells and carry away the potentially toxic

wastes of the metabolic activity that maintains life. Closely aligned with the circulatory system is a system of lymphatic organs and vessels that provides a staging system for immune responses. The urinary system cleans the blood of impurities and manages the body's "internal sea" of water, salts and other substances.

Reproductive systems provide the biological means for producing offspring. Controlling and regulating every aspect of body functioning are the hormones of the endocrine system and the unparalleled human nervous system.

Wow!

In *Emotional Biochemistry*, Pilar Gerasimo says, "Like it or not, emotions share some very real biochemical links with your nervous, endocrine, immune and digestive systems. Isn't it time you learned something about how your body responds to what you feel and vice versa?" *Psycho* means mind. *Soma* means body. The term *psychosomatic*, which we've been taught to associate with *imaginary* illnesses, in fact refers to the physiological connection between the mind and body – a connection that is seemingly more concrete and evident by the day. Science is now showing us with increasing clarity our feelings and thoughts can help make us sick (or well) in a variety of ways that are definitely not "all in our head."

Laura Harris Smith is a certified nutritional counselor. In her book *The 30 Day Faith Detox*, she list fifteen body systems:
  * digestive (mouth, esophagus, stomach, liver, large intestines);
  * excretory (small intestines, colon, rectum);
  * urinary (kidneys, bladder, gallbladder);
  * respiratory (nose, lungs, pharynx, larynx, trachea, bronchi, alveoli);
  * immune (bone marrow, thymus, glands);
  * lymphatic (spleen, lymph nodes, ducts, tonsils);
  * endocrine (hypothalamus, pituitary, thyroid, adrenals, pineal body);
  * nervous (brain, spinal cord, nerves);
  * reproductive (ovaries, testes);
  * cardiovascular (heart, blood vessels: arteries, capillaries, veins);
  * circulatory (blood, all vessels);
  * integumentary (skin, hair, nails, sweat glands);
  * skeletal (bones, bone marrow, joints, teeth, ligament, cartilage);
  * muscular (muscles).
  * sensory (sight, hearing, feeling, smelling, testing and balance)

Man did not create the human body. God did. As knowledgeable as they are, doctors can't possibly know all there is to know about its workings. If we focused on just one part of the human body, we can see how detailed God's handiwork is. For instance, I have learned the liver is a remarkable organ. It must be in good working order to maintain a healthy immune system. The way we think will impact its effectiveness.

The bottom line is that God is truly the Great Physician. Exodus 15:26 (NIV) reminds us that if we want to be well, we must choose the thoughts, relationships, and behaviors that keep us in right alignment with God, who created us. There is absolutely a connection between our thoughts, emotions, and health. As I completed the personal inventory, I was able to gain some clarity about how my thoughts impacted my health. I have listed three examples here.

1. **Thoughts:** I was thinking there is no way to fix this. I will have to be on medication for life. This made me very sad. I constantly had feelings of hopelessness and living in a state of constant loss. The emotions I had most were: unrest, anxiety, fear, and frustration (Satan's system-of-delivery).
    Spiritual Root Cause: I was unable to rest in God's ability to intervene in my life.
    Physical Manifestation: High blood pressure (a preexisting condition).
    Objective: Homeostasis (God's system-of-delivery)
    Personal Choice: Investigate and learn how to be proactive about my health and my relationship with God.

2. **Thoughts:** I thought if I could research this problem, maybe I could find the solution. I discovered that I was dealing with consistent combinations of stress and unknowingly eating large quantities of natural blood thinners. Doctors said I had to be on medication for life. The emotions: Hope (God's system-of-delivery); unrest, fear, anxiety, depression (Satan's system-of-delivery)
    Spiritual Root Cause: I was unable to rest in God's ability to intervene in my life.
    Physical Manifestation: Chronic nose bleeds
    Objective: Homeostasis (God's system-of-delivery)
    Personal Choice: I can find and study my situation in the Bible. I can learn and do what I can to help myself. I can apply the information I learn.
    Because of doing my own research I discovered that the natural healing process was working, but the scab felt huge and uncomfortable. The slightest touch or movement would cause the newly formed scab to dislodge, and the bleeding would start again. I found an excellent article on the Johns Hopkins Medical Health and Library website titled "How Wounds Heal." The article goes on to say the process of healing is complicated and involves a long series of chemical signals to complete. I needed to learn how to work with the chemical signals.

    I learned that paprika, thyme, garlic, olive oil, cinnamon, dill, oregano, onions, licorice, peppermint, raisins, cherries, grapes, strawberries, tangerines, oranges, chewing gum, honey, peppermints, green tea, and lotion (for skin care) all have vitamin E. Vitamins are good, right? All of the things listed here are natural blood thinners. This was what I ate every day, sometimes two and three times or more for months. I thought I was making wise decisions based on my limited financial situation.

3. **Thoughts:** I thought that good things won't happen for me, but they do happen for other people. I had a poor understanding of how money worked. I felt ignorance, unrest, fear, anxiety, and depression (Satan's systems of delivery)
   Spiritual Root Cause: I was unable to rest in God's ability to intervene in my life.
   Physical Manifestation: Property loss.
   Objective: I want to secure a good understanding of how money really works as I rest in God's ability to work in my life, the lives of my family, and others (God's system of delivery).
   Personal Choice: I must find a way to learn and apply the information intentionally.
   Dr. David Malone is a science documentary film maker. He made a YouTube video called "Pure Science Specials—Of Hearts and Minds." It is imbedded in an article titled, "Modern Research Reveals Your Heart Does Have a Mind of Its Own." In it, David Paterson, a professor at Oxford University, says, "Neurons are what allow your brain to form thoughts. So what are they doing around the right ventricle of your heart? While much about the neurons in your heart is still unknown, one thing is sure—the 'brain' in your heart communicates back and forth with the brain in your head. It's a two-way street." Proverbs 4:23 says, "Above all else, guard your heart, for everything you do flows from it."

Memory in General

Out with the old and in with the new. Second Corinthians 5:17 (KJV) says, "Therefore, if any man be in Christ, he is a new creature: old things *are* passed away; all things *are* new."

Your memories (thoughts) are either supporting your growth or destroying your potential. Memory and forgiveness are closly related. You must connect with one in order to disconnect with the other. What you believe about who you are is embedded in your thoughts, and what you think is largely made up of where you've been, what you've done, and whom or what you've encountered.

Luke Mastin's diagram displays three types of memory stages—*sensory* (one second), *short-term* (working memory up to one minute), and *long-term* (lifetime) memory. Under long-term memory, he says the following: "*Explicit* (conscious), *Implicit* (unconscious), *Decla rative* (facts, events), *Procedural* (skills, tasks), *Episodic* (events, experiences) and *Sematic* (facts, concepts)." If you would like to see the diagram and read his article on this fascinating subject, google, Luke Mastin's, Types of Memory-The Human Memory.

Resting is another important step in maintaining health. A lack of rest can give us mood swings, shorten our tempers, and make us more likely to make poor decisions. If we are not careful, it can lead to serious health issues.

It seems to me God wants His people to be in a resting mode, knowing (depending on the fact) He is able to do exceedingly abundantly above all we ask or think, according to the power that works in us for all generations. To God be the glory (Ephesians 3:20-21 NIV).

I wanted to know what Jesus Christ had to say about the Sabbath. Matthew 12:11 (KJV) says, "And he said unto them, 'What man shall there be among you, that shall have one sheep, and if it falls into a pit on the Sabbath day, will he not lay hold on it and lift it out?'" Luke 6:1-11 (NIV) says,

> One Sabbath Jesus was going through the grain fields, and His disciples began to pick some heads of grain, rub them in their hands and eat the kernels. Some of the Pharisees asked, "Why are you doing what is unlawful on the Sabbath?" Jesus answered, "Have you never read what David did when he and his companions were hungry?"
>
> He entered the house of God and taking the consecrated bread, he ate what is lawful only for priests to eat. And he also gave some to his companions." Then Jesus said to them, "The Son of Man is Lord of the Sabbath." On another Sabbath he went into the synagogue and was teaching, and a man was there whose right hand was shriveled. The Pharisees and the teachers of the law were looking for a reason to accuse Jesus, so they watched Him closely to see if He would heal on the Sabbath. But Jesus knew what they were thinking and said to the man with the shriveled hand, "Get up and stand in front of everyone." So he got up and stood there.
>
> Then Jesus said to them, "I ask you, which is lawful on the Sabbath: to do good or to do evil, to save life or to destroy it?" He looked around at them all and said to the man, "Stretch out your hand." He did so and his hand was completely restored. But the Pharisees and teachers of the law were furious and began to discuss with one another what they might do to Jesus.

I rested, keeping the Sabbath. Exodus 31:13 (NIV) says "Say to the Israelites, 'You must observe My Sabbaths. This will be a sign between Me and you for generations to come, so you may know I am the LORD, Who makes you holy'" Mark 2:27 (NIV) says, "Then He (Jesus) said to them, 'The Sabbath was made for man, not man for the Sabbath.'" I decided to apply this word to my life, and I have been truly blessed because of it.

God rested on the seventh (Sabbath) day, sanctified it, and made it holy (Genesis 2:2–3 NIV). Therefore, I submit that God created the Sabbath day of rest for everyone. It was much later in history when God told Moses to tell the Israelites to "*remember* the Sabbath day (seventh day) to keep it holy" (Exodus 20:8 NIV). Then God told Moses to tell them *how* to keep it holy. "And the seventh day is the Sabbath (seventh day) of the LORD your God; in it you shall not do any work, nor your son, your daughter, your manservant, nor your maidservant, nor your cattle, nor your stranger who is within your gates" (Exodus 20:10 NIV).

"Six days you shall do your work, and on the seventh day you shall rest: that your ox and donkey may rest, and the son of your handmaid, and the stranger, may be refreshed" (Exodus 23:12). God says to speak also to the children of Israel, saying, "Verily My Sabbaths you shall keep: for it is a sign between Me and you throughout your generations; that you may know I am the LORD Who sanctifies you" (Exodus 31:13 NIV). "You shall keep My Sabbaths and reverence My Sanctuary: I am the LORD," (Leviticus 19:30 NIV).

In summary, the Sabbath is a day of rest for family fellowship, relationship/community building, and Bible study. We are not to cause anyone to buy, sell, or work on the Sabbath. People and animals alike are supposed to rest. God says, "Speak to the children, telling them the Sabbath of God will keep them." to keep the Sabbath because it is a sign, a symbol, a signal, a mark between Him and the people throughout their generations. I have come to believe this sign is to the believer and the nonbeliever.

I have been reading articles and books as well as watching documentaries and specials—everything I can find that has to do with regaining, restoring, or acquiring health as it pertains to the Sabbath day connection. I was interested in knowing both the benefits and the hardships associated with it. What I was learning about these connections inspired me to start keeping the Sabbath. I asked the Holy Spirit to teach me what I needed to know. John 14:26 says, "But the Comforter, which is the Holy Ghost, Whom the Father will send in My Name, He shall teach you all things, and bring all things to your remembrance, whatsoever I have said unto you."

The Sabbath is not a religion or just another activity. It is highly personal, introspective and intentionally designed to commune with God while our bodies and mindes refreshed. It also sets God (Yahweh) apart from everything else. It becomes crystal clear He is being worshipped on this day. He is the one and only true and living God, the author and Creator of the Sabbath day.

My Sabbath Day's Journey Experience.

A. **Sabbath Day Experience #1:** I had a restful day and was looking forward to the next one. I researched information on keeping the Sabbath. I had my bible and meals ready and canceled all other functions. I intended to rest, pray, read, and study the Bible; spend time with my husband and children and maybe watch a Christian movie. I opened the Bible and ended up eating and sleeping most of the time. I slept most of the time and began to realize this was going to take a lot of planning. I was disappointed I did not study more or spend time with my family. My husband was kind enough to let me sleep. He checked in with me occasionally to see if I needed anything. I had no idea I was actually that tired and rundown. Saturday is usually a very busy day for most people. If I wanted to connect with someone, Saturday was the day most people wanted to schedule. I had invitations to do things during this time, but I declined.

B. **Sabbath Day Experience #2:** Another restful day. Not much went on. The week was very busy. During the day I practiced taking my thoughts captive by comparing them to what the scriptures said about them (see 2 Corinthians 10:5 NKJV). I wanted to study, rest, relax, fellowship with family members and others as we talk about the things of God and learn more about Him. Again, I slept most of the time. It was almost the same as the first Sabbath day. I felt like I let God down by sleeping so much but I was happy about actually feeling rested for a change. I hadn't known that feeling in a long time. **Note on thoughts:** If a thought generates negative feelings/emotions, hopelessness, irresponsibility, anger, worry, fear, regret, or revenge, it is *condemnation* and not from God. It is debilitating and destructive. Reject it. Don't think on it. Seek wisdom concerning it. If a thought generates feelings/emotions in agreement with how the Word of God says they should be handled (e.g., repentant, accountable, hopeful, fact-finding, problem-solving, etc.), it is a thought of *conviction* and is from God. It will be restorative and full of potential healing. Accept it. Think on it.

C. **Sabbath Day Experience #3:** I prayed and asked God for wisdom, understanding, direction, and clarity. I did all of the cleaning, shopping, and errands before the seventh day of the week began. I had scripture readings, topics, and Bible study materials already picked out. I prepared to enjoy the day, and I was ready to be approachable if necessary. I intended to spend time in prayer, rest, relax, and fellowship with family members and others as we talked about the things of God and learned more about Him. I got up early. I prayed for a while. I interceded as the Holy Spirit led me. Read the Bible. I gave myself permission to allow my mind and body to relax and rest in the Lord fully, excepting to be restored. The day was full of good rest, fellowshipping in person and on the phone, and lots of laughing. I agreed to help out with an event for a limited amount of time. I kept my word and left on time. This was a good day.

D. **Sabbath Day Experience #4:** I had already made my Preparation. The day is already set aside. While I told precious few what I was doing, it was becoming common knowledge that getting me to engage in anything on the Sabbath day would not be easy. I intended to study, pray, rest, relax, and fellowship with family members and others as we talk about the things of God and learn more about Him. I picked up a few things from the store on the seventh day (Sabbath) and ate at a restaurant. I did some studying and fellowshipping with the Lord.

I have researched the connection between rest and healing, and I have experienced both along the way. It turns out God knows exactly what He's talking about. I was not trying to start a movement. I had no need to convince anyone to do this with me. This was strictly between God and me. I wanted to experience this Sabbath journey and see what happened. It was one of the best decisions I ever made, and I will continue to learn about and keep the Sabbath.

In short, I believe we are fearfully and wonderfully made. God did create, us and His works are wonderful. The human body *is* the most complex and unique organism in the world, and that complexity and uniqueness speaks volumes about the mind and ability of our Creator. This leads me to conclude that we must follow our Creator's guidelines to live well.

The **chart on the next page is** an example of how I believe thoughts can impact relationship connections that impact our lives daily. How would you describe the impact your thoughts are having on your life?

The Chemical Response to Personal Thought Diagram below is an example of how I believe thoughts can impact relationship connections that impact our lives daily. How would you describe the impact your thoughts are having on your life?

Chemical Response to Personal Thought Diagram
A thought comes into your mind
(conscious or unconscious).
↓

An automatic chemical response is triggered.
↓

The thoughts you think automatically signal your brain to release chemicals that will impact your body in positive or negative ways.
As a result, the
designated chemicals are released internally, and you will continue to experience or come to be in in a constant state of one of the following:

<u>Homeostasis</u>	or	<u>Unrest</u>
Security		Insecurity
Peacefulness		Anxiousness
Boldness		Fear
Hopefulness		Hopelessness
Joyfulness		Depression
A steady state		Disturbance
Rest, poise, balance		Upheaval
Steadiness, stability		Rioting

which produces
(Healing/Wellness/Peace)   or   (Disease/Disease)
which will put you or keep you in agreement with:

God's system of delivery   or   Satan's system of delivery
(Kingdom of Heaven)   (Kingdom of Darkness)

v.

With which kingdom does your relationship connections, thoughts and feelings keep your health in agreement?
Should you keep, stop, or change things?

Forgiveness

Does

Not

Mean

You

Don't

Have

Boundaries.

Forgiveness is the power to let go, disconnect, and move on in a positive state of mind.

Learn the lesson and leave the trash behind.

Chapter 5

Relationship Connections

Plan how to include and apply the Word of God in all of your decisions.

Pray often. Ask people you know who are serious about prayer to pray for you as you walk and stand in faith. Ask God to give you and your family the information needed to be well in every area of your lives. Some days will be better than others, but God will see you through. Pray that He becomes more real to you than ever before.

Study the Bible, stay physically active, and help others. Implement new information (with wisdom) as soon as you can. Implement changes in simple and consistent ways until you receive a break-through on a day-by-day basis. Sometimes you may have to start over, but stay the course.

Take every thought captive. Inventory your lifestyle choices in a way that can bring clarity and direction. Second Corinthians 10:5 (KJV) says, "Casting down imaginations and every high thing that exalts itself against the knowledge of God, bringing into captivity every thought to the obedience of Christ."

Make a conscious decision to *give* your whole heart to Jesus and seek the face of God in every area of your life, to *grow* in your knowledge of the Bible, and to *invest* in your uniquely personal relationship with the God who set you here for a time such as this. Deuteronomy 31:6 (NIV) says, "Be strong and courageous. Do not be afraid or terrified because of them, for the LORD your God goes with you; He will never leave you, nor forsake you."

Remember God was always speaking. Remember to listen. Keep prayer as an automatic response to every situation. Isaiah 65:24 says, "KJV) says, "Before they call I will answer; while they are still speaking I will hear."

Identify three triggers drawing you into the situation or problem. Decide how you will deal with them. Make a reasonable plan that you can actually accomplish. Keep your plan simple. Continue to study the scriptures you've researched as you go through the process. Pick people who can and will support your accountability process. They will encourage you, but you must do the work, take the stand, and accept responsibility for your actions and correction with sensitivity and love.

Write down the first three stages of your plan.
 1.
 2.
 3.

What will be your response to the trigger(s) you have identified?
 1.
 2.
 3.

List at least one person you respect and can count on as you go through this process. Idealistically, he or she will be a person whose trust you have already earned and has already earned yours. Pick just one to start. Create well-defined boundaries to which both of you can agree. Showing love, respect, appreciation, and forgiveness for each other during this time is most important. Praying for and with each other is also key.

When you are ready, create a plan for the following:
 • giving,
 • fasting,
 • resting,
 • staying accountable,
 • setting well-defined boundaries for relationships,
 • studying,
 • praying,
 • sharing the gospel, and
 • reevaluating.

Chapter 6

Scriptures and Steps to aid in maintaining application strategies.

Don't forget to watch your lifestyle choices, your connections systems of delivery, and interpretation of doctrine closely (1 Timothy 4:16 NLV).

There is always a root cause and reason why we do the things we do. You must do the following:

Accept Jesus Christ. "If you declare with your mouth, 'Jesus is Lord,' and believe in your heart God raised Him from the dead, you will be saved" (Romans 10:9 NIV).

Repent of known sin. "Repent, then and turn to God, so your sins may be wiped out, that times of refreshing may come from the Lord" (Acts 3:19 NIV).

"*Renounce* the things hidden which have caused shame and don't indulge in them anymore because they are craftiness or adulterating to the Word of God" (1 John 4:2 NIV).

Destroy or get rid of occult objects, including books, jewelry, games, music, etc., (Acts 19:19 NIV).

Remove and turn from Satan. Dissociate yourself from the place, things, events, or people (in a safe way) that draw you back into the sin you are walking away from (2 Corinthians 6:14–16 NIV).

Rest in Christ's deliverance "because He delivered us from the domain of the darkness and transferred us to the Kingdom of His Beloved Son" (Colossians 1:13–14 NIV).

Resist. Don't go back. Get the help and support you need to keep yourself in a right relationship with God and others (James 4:1–10 NIV).

Renew your mind. Think the thoughts that will keep you strong with God (Philippians 4:1–9 NIV).

Pray with others. The Bible says that *if* two (corporate prayer) of you agree on earth about anything you may ask, "it shall be done by My Father who is in Heaven." We must remember the thing being asked must agree with the Word of God. God will not answer prayers for the ill will of another (Matthew 18.19 NIV).

Fellowship. They devoted themselves to the apostles' teaching, fellowship, the breaking of bread, and prayer (Acts 2:42 NIV).

Rejoice. Give God thanks for setting you free, and enjoy your freedom (1 Thessalonians 5:16–18 NIV).

When you fall short of a goal, get back up, dust yourself off, and begin again. It's a path we all must travel. One day you will find you have made it. You can do all things through Christ who strengthens you. (Philippians 4:13 NKJV).

Chapter 7

Prayer, Prophecy, Dream, and Vision Journals

Next. God wants us to be informed, equipped, engaged, stabilized and directed by Him.

God, informs, warns, and equips His people for whatever is coming next. The rest is up to them.

Here are just a few examples.

The Flood—God gave Noah instructions. Noah told the people the flood was coming (Genesis 6:1-22 NIV).

The Famine—God gave Pharaoh two dreams. Pharaoh told Joseph. Joseph prayed for understanding. God gave Joseph understanding, and Joseph explained it to Pharaoh (Genesis 41:28-32 NIV).

Destruction of Sodom and Gomorrah—God sent two angels to tell Lot. Lot tried to warn his family and others (Genesis 19:12-14 NIV).

A King Will Oppress the People. God told Samuel, and Samuel told the people (1 Samuel 8:6-19 NIV).

Abomination of Desolation—God gave King Nebuchadnezzar a dream. The king called for his advisors to tell him the meaning of the dream, but they could not. Daniel heard what happened and turned to God and received the meaning. God gave Daniel the meaning, and Daniel explained it to the king (Daniel 2 NIV; Matthew 24:15-22 NIV; Mark 13:14-20 NIV).

The Man of Lawlessness—God gave visions to the apostle Paul. Paul wrote 2 Thessalonians, and that's what you are reading today (2 Thessalonians 2:1-16 NIV).

The Destruction of the Temple and Signs of the End Times—The disciples asked Jesus to tell them the signs of the end times. Jesus reminded them that God had already sent the answer to that question through the prophet Daniel. Peter and Matthew wrote it, down and you can read about the events today. Mark may not have been in that group of disciples, but he was given most of his book from Peter (Mark 13:3-35 NIV).

God is talking to you right now through the pages of the Holy Bible. What directives or warnings has He given you, your family, your church, and others?

Prayer: "Prayer is man giving God permission to get involved in the affairs of man." I really like this statement made by Dr. Myles Munroe. Matthew 6:5–14 (NIV) says,

And when you pray, do not be like the hypocrites, for they love to pray standing in the synagogues and on the street corners to be seen by others. Truly I tell you, they have received their reward in full. But when you pray, go into your room, close the door and pray to your Father, Who is unseen. Then your Father, Who sees what is done in secret, will reward you. And when you pray, do not keep on babbling like pagans, for they think they will be heard because of their many words. Do not be like them, for your Father knows what you need before you ask Him. This, then, is how you should pray: 'Our Father in Heaven, hallowed be Your Name, Your Kingdom come, Your will be done on Earth as it is in Heaven. Give us today our daily bread and forgive us our debts, as we also have forgiven our debtors. Lead us not into temptation, but deliver us from the evil one.' For if you forgive other people when they sin against you, your heavenly Father will also forgive you. But if you do not forgive others their sins, your Father will not forgive your sins.

Dream/Prophecy and Vision Journal
Read Amos 3:7 (NKJV) and Acts 2:17 (NKJV) "Surely the LORD God does nothing, unless He reveals His secret to His servants the prophets. And it shall come to pass afterward, I will pour out My spirit upon all flesh; your *sons* and *daughters* shall prophesy, your *old men* shall dream dreams, your *young men* shall see visions."

Here are some entries from my journal. Don't forget to record the dreams, prophecies and visions that God gives to you in yours.

Log Entries

On 3/12/09
I was in prayer, and I felt impressed to write the words that came into my heart.

Hide and seek is what happens during deliverance. In the game, the only way you know someone is hiding behind a chair, door, or shelf is if you detect movement. In the case of deliverance, the body is the hiding place, and the movement is the manifestation.

Fasting is to the spirit what detoxing is to the body. They both release and expel impurities pollution and toxins, one from the (spirit) and the other from the body (flesh). Once the impurities and toxins are expelled, you must supply the proper nourishment to strengthen and keep both healthy. This event is designed to build both immune systems at the same time. This process brings revelation to the mind and cleans the body, the spirit and the flesh.

On 10/30/2009 at 5:35 a.m.
I was in prayer, and I felt impressed to write the words that came into my heart.

God woke me by saying," Get up. They are praying!" I knew exactly what He was referring to. I got out of bed and called the prayer line from my phone. Last week when I was on the prayer line, the Lord kept talking to me about a voice of many waters. As I listened to the intercessors call out to God, I became aware of how strong and different their voices sounded. This morning I had the same experience, so I asked God what I needed to understand about the voices of many waters. I searched my Bible concordance, and Revelation 19:6 (NIV) jumped out at me. I stayed engaged with the prayer, interceding along with my coworkers in Christ and rereading Revelation 1:15 N(IV). It said, "And His feet were like burnished bronze, when it has been caused to glow in the furnace and His voice was like the sound of many waters."

God began to speak to my spirit, saying, "This is the standard I am building throughout the land. My standard is being raised through prayer. I am so pleased right now. People ask Me if I can hear them. Think about this moment in time. Everyone on this phone is calling out to Me one at a time and of one accord. Just like you can recognize and pick out the voices of people on this call, so can I when My people call on Me. You can't see each other, but you still recognize one another's voices distinctively. I see you clearly, and I marvel at this sound in heaven because it is the voice of My Word coming back to Me. It's the voice of My Word. My voice, the voice of many waters." I am moved by this.

On 7/25/99
I was in prayer about Sunday service, seeking understanding.

God said, "Be prepared to trust Me blindly. Not a person, just Me and My leading. Know the Spirit that is dealing with you. I am breaking off trust and blind trust in man's ability. You have been asking for My Spirit to have His way with this body of Christ. Satan sees what is Mine and counterfeits it. By what measure do you determine if it is Me or the counterfeiter? You ask Me for deeper things, a deeper manifestation of My Spirit. Deeper things require a deeper walk. What measure of time have you dwelt with Me individually? What measure of time are you willing to dwell with Me right now? How well can you really know Me, My character, My love, and My ability if you don't seek My face continually?

"The end times are swiftly approaching. The battle will be great, and deception will run rampant. False Christs and false prophets will arise and will show great signs and wonders so as to mislead (if possible) even the elect (Matthew 24:24 KJV). If you abide in My Word, then you are truly disciples of Mine. You shall know the truth and the truth shall make you free.

"False Christs and prophets will target My people in leadership and intentionally mislead, disrupt, and divide them if it is at all possible. They will attempt this even if the possibility is slight."

The word *beguiled* keeps coming into my mind. Beguiled means to mislead by cheating or tricking. God told me to look back over the last two weeks, so I retraced my steps in my mind. I was very busy and did not consult with God. Consult means to call, to gather or ask for advice. I was preoccupied with things. As a result, my guard was down. In order for people to be beguiled, a certain mind-set or door must be opened.

For example, Hitler could not have done what he did if the climate was not right for it to happen. The people were not on guard. They felt like society would not allow him to prevail. The people (even many of the Jewish people) did not believe the events that took place could ever happen to them. Many felt safe, but while they were living their lives the best they could, Hitler was brainwashing people right before their eyes into believing and doing unspeakably wrong things. The people knew in their hearts these things were wrong, but by the time the truth became unmistakably evident, the situation was already in progress. People prayed, but the press came after the need. In other words, the people tried to stop it after it was already too late. People were looking out for their own individual interest and not consulting with God. They were misled by trickery. And so it is in the body of Jesus Christ. Who is praying?

The supernatural effect of being beguiled works like this. You see yourself doing a thing. You know it is not right, and you try to resist it on your own. Once you have been tricked (beguiled), the door is open for the spirit to move through it. Your will becomes neutralized, and you are moved beyond your own ability to control it. You go away, asking yourself, "Why did I do that? Why did I allow that to happen?" Even though you are aware of the thing that took place, you fail to see your part in it. This thing can only be broken by the power of God in the name of Jesus the Christ. Protect the anointing.

On 9/1/2010 at 6:30 a.m.
I was in prayer, and I felt impressed to write the words that came into my heart. I am speeding things up. God said to me, "Those who will be for Me will be for Me. Those who will be against Me will be against Me. You will know each other by your fruit. Men or women can say they love Me with their mouths but not love Me with their hearts. My people who are called by My name will humble themselves, and I will be with them. They shall recognize My presence and be comforted regardless of their circumstances, knowing I am able, alive, and well!"

On 8/17/2013 at 6:00 a.m.
God said, "Even Doppler (a weather radar tracking system to determine the location and velocity of a storm, clouds, and precipitation) is confused about what is going on with the weather. The god of this world has given pacifiers to the sleeping people. If they would just come to Me through My Word. Consider the ways of Daniel. Stay focused and get with those who seek My face. Whatever they are doing will confirm the truth if they are truly walking with God. Watch their ways and yours. When you get a word from God, look for the principle in the Bible. Talk about what it means and what it should look like when you walk it out.

On 9/29/2013 at 6:00 a.m.
God said, "We are in the last of the last days. Don't be afraid or double-minded. I have called you out of the world to be My witness. Some of you are in a holding place right now. Some of you are running so hard and fast I can't get your attention. Spend individual and personal time with Me so I can direct your path in the way you should go. All of the world is suffering. The birth pangs are being felt everywhere. I am coming soon. Make up your mind, and then live according to your choice because that is what God will judge you on. Consider these things: What are you doing? Where are you doing it? Who does it exalt? Do the people know of Me by your example?"

On 10/4/2013
I was in prayer, and I felt impressed to write the words that came into my heart.

The reason Jesus had to atone for our sins is because He had to create a way for man to participate with God that could not be corrupted by man. Atone means "to offset bad qualities with good."

On 12/27/2013
Dear reader, search your Bible and ask God yourself to confirm whether this is or is not His word.

I had a horrible dream. Never in my life have I had one like it. The evil present was not of this world. When I woke up, I got out of bed. I could not dream anymore, but the essence of it stayed with me. I rebuked the activities and demonic influence attached to the dream in the name of Jesus. As I began to pray in tongues, *these words came into my spirit, and I wrote them down.*

Intense evil is coming your way. Tell the people to give their lives to Jesus and seek the face of God. Then press for instruction and direction. I will not lead you into bondage but out of bondage. When the people went into bondage, it was by their own *choice* through *disobedience.* Disobedience to Me (God) is obedience to Satan. A man cannot serve two masters except if he hates one and loves the other.

In the dream I was telling a person that the angels of God could come and rescue us if they wanted. They could just come through the walls and take us out of here. At that very moment, for some reason unknown to me, I lost hope and said to them, "The angels are not coming, and my spirit is grieved." I then took my earrings off and put them under the mattress. I was in a prison cell. I had two sets of earrings on. The top earrings were small round posts, and the bottom earrings were small crosses. I knew in my heart one of the men in the dream wanted to break my will and cause me to renounce Jesus in front of the others. The plan was to publicly break the Christians down and take our testimonies at the same time. It was almost my turn. I started praying to God for help and continued praying as I woke up and entered into my morning prayer time.

The earrings I had on in the dream are the same ones I wear in real life. During this message God responded to what I said in the dream about the angels. "My angels do what I say. They already know what to do concerning those of you (My people) who are speaking My Word. My Word is both life and breath. Together they create a supernatural highway that supersedes everything natural and supernatural (demonic activity).

"Who is on their face calling to Me and listening to My voice? Did I not warn the people? The ones who would listen. *I am grieved because destruction is coming and My people are giving and taking in marriage and going to and fro as though they don't know the signs of the times.*

"Barak Obama is the new pharaoh. They look to him instead of Me. Others are looking to their Babylonian governments, not to Me. My Word says, 'They shall have their god, and the ones who look to Me shall have their God!' I have spoken on this matter through My Word. I have sent My Son, Jesus, to tell you. You are responsible for your own choices and eternal destination. I am beseeching you to choose Me. I love you, and I don't want you to parish."

Previous to this, I asked God why people lay prostrate when they pray. He answered, "The reason I have people lay prostrate, cover up, or go to their prayer closet when they pray is because I want them to close out *all* distractions. I am looking for intimacy between them and Me. People reject My prophets because I send My warnings through them. My prophets listen to Me. The people must know what the adversary is up to so they know how to avoid the traps. My people do not want to believe things they think are impossible because they think it will never happen to them, but it will! It has to if they don't heed My Word through the voice of My prophets. I will set you up and send you out. Open your mouth, and I will fill it. This is the Word of the Lord for you today."

On 2/18/2014 at 5:00 a.m.

About four o'clock this morning, the ringer on my husband's cell phone went off. His supervisor had sent the answer to a question he sent her the day before. Once it was clear there was no emergency, I tried to go back to sleep but could not rest. I got up to pray. This is what came into my spirit.

God said, "Soon every cell phone will spring to life, giving commands instead of receiving them. Time zones will not matter. Your geographic location will not make a difference. The call will go out, and you will be told to comply at once. The one thing all generations have in common is their dependence on the cell phone. You think you control the phone, but it really controls you. You pay for the service, but you are directed as to how much and how long you can use it. Isn't it true that once you purchase a thing, you should be the one to control its usage or fate? That's not so with the phone (technology). You were sold a solution to a problem and you became dependent upon it.

"Who does not need this phone service and can still be the great communicator? The great communicator (the Holy Spirit) can lead you into all truth and tell you what you need to know when you need to know it. Give your heart to Jesus and seek the face of God."

On 4/28/2014 at 5:47 a.m.

I was in prayer. I was repenting and asking God for forgiveness for not taking advantage of His opportunities (Matthew 25 NIV). Revelation and understanding came at 6:09 a.m. The Lord said, "What you take, you are responsible for. I don't do bailouts. I do reconciliation, revelation, and restoration. I am not a vending machine. I am a Father, and I love My children. I keep calling them to Me to come home through salvation. But My cries through My people are falling on deaf ears, and it's breaking My heart. I know what they must suffer for the choices they are making, but that was never My plan. But I must stay true to My Word and let them choose even though it is a hard thing to see. My people are fragmented, broken, and without direction. If they would only listen and obey, they would see and know the way out of everything that weighs them down. I am life-giving. I make the way out of no way. I show you what the traps are, where they are, how to avoid them, and what to do about them, but I won't move beyond your will for Me to do it. You must make the first step. Is it Me you have chosen or an idol carved from My creation?

"In Mark 1:4, John the Baptist called people out of the wilderness. That's why he was in the wilderness. I placed him where they could find him. The people were in the wilderness and they didn't even know it. Jesus showed them what happens when they come out of the wilderness. Once they took responsibility for being there, they could see clearly. They built relationships with Me. My power broke their bondage. They were delivered and made whole, and they learned about true love and right relationships.

"My heart is the same for the people today. I want them out of the wilderness. I want them delivered, healed, and in a right relationship with Me, but they won't let go of the deceiver's hand of provisions. What will it take? I am grieved to My soul. My people suffer for lack of knowledge because they are of a lazy and contrite heart. Tell them I am calling them to Me. I want to be their God, but the choice is theirs. And so are the consequences. I do love them. I did make them for a time such as this and for My glory. Tell them they are loved and wanted by Me."

On 5/2/14

In a dream I was sitting on a chair in what looked like a waiting room. I was looking up at a clock hanging on the wall directly in front of me. In the same room about two yards to my right, there were two chairs next to each other. A person was seated on each chair. Both of the people were also looking directly in front of them at the clock on the wall. Though I'm not sure who, someone said in a man's voice, "What time is it?" I said, "Five o'clock."

There were two men present, though I never saw them. I could only sense them. They sat in the chairs and said, "No, it's not. It's four o'clock."

I insisted it was five, and they insisted it was four. We began to argue. They became very upset with me and walked away, talking to each other about my not being able to discern the time correctly. I was still sitting in the chair, trying to understand how three people who were sitting in the same room at the same time and looking in the same direction and seeing the same clock could have such different opinions about what we were looking at. As I was still processing my thoughts, I stood up, walked over to where the other two were seated, and sat down in one of the chairs. I looked up at the clock and was greatly surprised by what I came to understand.

I discovered we were looking at two different clocks, but we *assumed* we were seeing the same thing. *The clock I was seeing was round with white trim and showed five o'clock. The clock they were seeing was square with purple trim and showed four o'clock.* Both clocks were about the same size. The clocks, the wall, the distance, and the placement of the chairs were deliberately set up that way. The purpose was to cause insecurity and misunderstanding, and that was exactly what happened with the people in the dream. The two walked away from the one.

Outcome #1: There was no agreement among the three.
Outcome #2: The agreement the two forged was based on insufficient information.
Outcome #3: Eventually I came to understand.

On 5/3/2014 at 7:00 a.m.

I was in prayer, asking God to explain the dream I just had. I didn't know how to write the dream down because it was so complicated. The following are the words I felt inspire to write:

In the coming days, deception will be so great that the people will look and think they are seeing the same thing. They will not be aware that they are actually witnessing different things at the same time. The things will be so similar that the understanding of the individuals will be divided because each of them will think their perception is the correct one.

The only way the people will know they have been intentionally deceived is by taking the time to slow down, verbally compare what they think they are seeing, and be willing to accept the truth of it. *People are seeing the counterfeit, explaining it as if it's reality, and accepting it as truth.* Good friends, close friends, and loved ones will second-guess one another because they will each think they are the only ones seeing and understanding clearly. Then the people will turn on one another, trusting in their own soundness of mind and their own opinions. Each one will think they are right, but they will believe a lie.

"Oh, find Me now beloved! Come running with all of your might. Leave it all and give your life to Jesus before He comes back, because when you see Him it will be too late!"

Second Thessalonians 2 (NIV) says, "The only way I can tell My people what they need to know, is if they come to Me and are willing to wait for the answer and direction I need to give them."

"Tell them to practice lack and take care of what they have while they have the choice, so when their needs are met, when they get more, they can be well. The provisions I send their community are not just for the individual. Prepare for hard times, be ready to live and die for Me and remember I am with you always. Tell the people to spend time with Me; judgment has already been released (Philippians 4:19 NIV; Matthew 6:6 NIV).

"Ask them these questions: Who am I to you? Where is the love I left as your inheritance? I left it to you at the cross. What are you doing with it? Who are you caring for and loving in My Name? Will I recognize you when we meet on Judgment Day or will I say to you, 'depart from Me, I never knew you.'? Will I say to you, 'Go to the right and/or to the left.'? You can know the answer to these questions right now. The answer is in My Word" (Luke 9:20 NIV; Ephesians 1:11 NIV; Matthew 7:23; 25:33 NIV; 2 Timothy 2:15 NIV).

On 5/15/14 at 5:08

I was in prayer. The following came into my heart, and I wrote it down:

God said, "I will come to you in the midnight hour and tell you many things. You will have to move quickly, the same pull on your heart to come close to Me, I have put on the hearts of others, but the cares of this world have won most of them over. Take swift and immediate action. You will know for sure which direction is from Me and which is not."

On 7/8/2014

I was in prayer, and I felt impressed to write the words that came into my heart.

I had a dream. The day was so beautiful. The sky was the most perfect blue. The weather was perfect. There was no need for a jacket. I saw a long, wide bridge. It arched over a large body of water. There was not a ripple in the water. It was calm, peaceful, and lovely. There was a group of people (elders) working together to move a table from one end of the bridge to the other. I thought it was a fold-up table, but it wasn't. I took a closer look, and there were no legs on it. About six or seven adults were trying different hand positions to move the tabletop.

I was trying to tell the people to look up. I wanted them to know while everything seemed perfect, things were going to change quickly, and they needed to be ready. They were hyper focused on the tabletop, so I decided to help. I thought that if I could help them get the table where they wanted it to be, they would listen to me. I went to help lift the table, and I was surprised when I was able to lift it by myself. I put the tabletop (or what looked like a tabletop) down on the opposite end of the bridge.

When I put it down the elders immediately began trying to pick it up and take it back to where they had started. I could not believe my eyes. I looked around, and there were groups of people doing the same things repeatedly. They were complacent and content. I was so sad because there was no emotional connection, just toiling.

Paris E. Moore

On 10/12/14 at 6:30 a.m.

I was in prayer, and God said, "Say to the people, 'Everything you take for granted now will become precious in the days to come. Less is more. Pray and reach the people. Bring them into the ark through salvation. Tell them about Noah. Noah never heard of rain, yet he knew Me. And My Word is the Word.

"Noah endured abuse until the day of judgment when I closed the door to the task that I set on My servant's heart 120 years before the judgment was to come to pass. During that time, Noah was telling the people of the coming *rain*. If even one of them trusted My Word and took My Word seriously like Noah did, they would have been in the ark too (Genesis 7:16; 18:24–32 NIV).

"Ask them whose word they are trusting. Tell them judgment is on the way because the United States is a stiff-necked nation. If My people, who are called by My name, will humble themselves, pray, seek My face, and turn from their wicked ways, then I will hear from heaven. I will forgive their sin and will heal their land" (2 Chronicles 7:14 NIV). Tell them they will be impacted by things they can't even imagine because they chose not to heed My warnings. When the time comes, each person will pledge allegiance to Me or an idol (2 Timothy 3:1 NIV; Revelation 3:10 13:17 NIV; 2 Thessalonians 2:9–10 NIV).

Some of them will become so hungry that they will sell their birthright for food. Others will be so overwhelmed by the need of others (a child, mother, father, sister, brother, or friend), they will take the mark of the beast so they can buy and sell. This will hurt My heart, but I must allow them a free choice (Revelation 13:16–17 NIV; Ephesians 4:29–32 NIV). The choice is to do or not do as I have said. You can choose to follow My Word and accept the consequences associated with it or not follow My Word and accept those consequences. You are free agents, and you can choose where you will spend eternity.

"I send warnings through—the heavens (Joel 2:30–32 NIV), the Bible (Hebrews 11:7), my prophets (2 Chronicles 36:15 NIV), dreams, visions (Job 33:15–18 NIV), and more. I want My people to hear My Words and live by them. I don't want to send judgments, but I must respond to the actions of the people. Say to them again, 'If My people who are called by My name will humble themselves, pray, seek My face, and *turn* from their wicked ways, then I will hear from heaven, I will forgive their sin and will heal their land (2 Chronicles 7:14 NIV; Joshua 24:15 NIV).

"Woe to the churches not teaching My people how to stand in these last days. They must be prepared in mind, body, and soul to say *no* to Babylon and *yes* to Me. My prophets told the people how to stand. Jesus taught and showed them how to stand. Noah withstood even when he was surrounded by much evil and unbelief. Rahab trusted Me during an impossible situation in her life, and eleven of the disciples withstood in their evil day unto death. Will you withstand too?" (1 Timothy 4:1 NIV; 1 Peter 5:9 NIV; Ephesians 6:13 NIV).

Withstand means (a) to stand against, to oppose with firm determination, especially to resist successfully, and (b) to be proof against, resist the effect of, withstand the impact of a landing to stop or obstruct the course of.

The Ark: If Noah was 480 years old when God told him to build an ark and six hundred when the flood came, it is reasonable to assume the construction of the ark took place during this 120-year period (see Genesis 6:3 NIV along with 1 Peter 3:20 NIV).

Note: A week or so ago during my prayer time, I asked God to heal everyone all over the world. He said He would not do that because if He did, the people would be confused and think their idols had done it. The people must be clear where their blessings come from.

On 1/15/15

This came to my spirit as I was waking up. God said, "Where is your dependence and hope for possibilities? Is it in the plans of man or the hands of God? It can't be both ways. Practice abstinence of everything and have all things in moderation and to the glory of God. Build an altar to Me in your heart. An altar of love and humility. Then live that way. Use the Bible as your ruler and the Holy Spirit as your guide."

Then I saw in my mind the image of a gyroscope. God continued, "A time is coming when you won't know what to do except as Jesus directs you. You must know Him for yourself. Do not depend on others to know Who He is. If you can't receive the knowledge for yourself, you won't be able to act on it. There won't be time to get somebody else's opinion.

Everything is happening even faster for both the wheat and the tares, the good and the bad. I am the only navigator who can save your soul. Learn to receive from Me now! Learn the difference between My voice and the voice of an imposter, and I will guide you into all righteousness. My people are crying out, asking where the signs and wonders from Me are. Tell them they are truly there among you."

On 12/31/15 at 7:30 p.m.

God said, "Everything is coming to a head. You need to be vested in the God you serve. If you don't already know how to stand in the shadow of the Almighty, it will be almost impossible to do so. The counterfeit deception of the adversary will look so close to My authentic that without the evidence found in the Word of God, you will be left unsure, unprotected, and confused.

"Drop everything and come to Me with your whole heart, soul, and mind. Everything and every group you know about is trying to get their needs met without Me. No longer! Nothing you have is worth anything unless it's directed by Me.

"Live for Me now. Everyone is appointed to die once. Don't be afraid. Be at peace. I have already made a way for you. I am with you always.

"Do I love you? Yes. Do I love you? Yes. Yes, yes, yes. A thousand times yes! Live your life for Me and allow everyone to make the same choice. Be serious and steadfast, and obey My Word.

Second Timothy 3:1 (KJV) says, "This know also, that in the last day's perilous times shall come." Read all of 2 Timothy (KJV).

Proverbs 3:5–6 (KJV) says, "Trust in the LORD with all thine heart; and lean not unto thine own understanding. In all thy ways acknowledge him, and he shall direct thy paths. Be not wise in thine own eyes: fear the LORD, and depart from evil."

Psalm 91:1–2 (KJV) says, "He that dwelleth in the secret place of the most-High shall abide under the shadow of the Almighty. 2 I will say of the LORD, He is my refuge and my fortress: my God; in him will I trust."

First Timothy 4:1–10 (KJV) says, I charge thee therefore before God, and the Lord Jesus Christ, who shall judge the quick and the dead at his appearing and his kingdom; Preach the word; be instant in season, out of season; reprove, rebuke, exhort with all long suffering and doctrine. For the time will come when they will not endure sound doctrine; but after their own lusts shall they heap to themselves teachers, having itching ears; And they shall turn away their ears from the truth, and shall be turned unto fables. But watch thou in all things, endure afflictions, do the work of an evangelist, make full proof of thy ministry. For I am now ready to be offered, and the time of my departure is at hand. I have fought a good fight, I have finished my course, I have kept the faith: Henceforth there is laid up for me a crown of righteousness, which the Lord, the righteous judge, shall give me at that day: and not to me only, but unto all them also that love his appearing. Do thy diligence to come shortly unto me: For Demas hath forsaken me, having loved this present world, and is departed unto Thessalonica; Crescens to Galatia, Titus unto Dalmatia.

First Timothy 2:15 (KJV) says, "Study to shew thyself approved unto God, a workman that needeth not to be ashamed, rightly dividing the word of truth."

Mark 8:36–38 (KJV) says, "For what shall it profit a man, if he shall gain the whole world, and lose his own soul? Or what shall a man give in exchange for his soul? Whosoever therefore shall be ashamed of me and of my words in this adulterous and sinful generation; of him also shall the Son of man be ashamed, when he cometh in the glory of his Father with the holy angels."

Hebrews 9:27 (KJV) says, "And as it is appointed unto men once to die, but after this the judgment."

Philippians 4:7 (KJV) says, "And the peace of God, which passeth all understanding, shall keep your hearts and minds through Christ Jesus."

Isaiah 43:19 (KJV) says, "Behold, I will do a new thing; now it shall spring forth; shall ye not know it? I will even make a way in the wilderness, and rivers in the desert."

John 3:16–17 (KJV) says, "For God so loved the world, that he gave his only begotten Son, that whosoever believeth in him should not perish, but have everlasting life. For God sent not his Son into the world to condemn the world; but that the world through him might be saved."

On 2/1/16

In my dream I saw people continuing to play and go on vacation while others were experiencing destruction at that very moment.

When I woke up, I heard the Lord say, "Go to Isaiah 47:1." I got up and read Isaiah 47:1–15 (NIV). Isaiah 47:11 (NIV) described exactly what I saw happening in my dream. At about 4:00 a.m., I was praying because I was overwhelmed by the conditions of the people's hearts. They seemed to be oblivious to the reality that was impacting them. I felt impressed by the Lord to write the following words from God: "I am setting a stage for you, daughter. Tell the people I said, 'Isaiah 47. All of it.' Warn them I am coming and to repent! Tell them to check their hearts. Tell them every life is at stake. The color of their skin cannot save them. It will be a burden to them no matter where they go because people will be of a desolate heart. But I say to you and them, read Isaiah 48:9 (NIV): For My name's sake, I will defer My anger, and for My praise, I will restrain it from you so that I do not cut you off."

Note that *desolate* means to unleash physical destruction as in a war; to destroy, ruin, devastate, lay waste, ravage, havoc. This definition absolutely described what I saw in my dream.

The Dream

I was at a hospital with a friend who lived for the Lord. She helped new mothers at the hospital. The hospital was in great shape. Everything was clean, and the staff was helpful. While we were there, a state of emergency was announced. I don't know what happened to my friend, but the hospital began to morph into different types of scenery. The floor of the hospital began to break up, and everything turned gray in color. I was also watching someone else run for her life.

When the people with white skin had the upper hand, many of the other people with white skin did too. The surroundings began to deteriorate with every step of the dream. When the people with darker skin tones had the upper hand, many of the people with the same skin tones did too. No one fully trusted anyone. Everyone was trying to find something they needed. They were looking for safety, but there was none to be found.

The last scene I saw was a beautiful sight at first. It looked like a warm summer day. The water was a beautiful blue. The beach was clean, sandy, and dotted with people playing and enjoying themselves. It was as though I was looking at the people through a picture frame. I was looking at this young man (whom I knew) riding past me on a jet ski. It looked as though he was coming so close to me I could reach out and touch him. I saw a big smile on his face, and at that same moment, I became aware of an overwhelming disaster. It all happened so fast. It was as though I saw the man and the approaching disaster at the same time. The scene changed quickly, and so did the atmosphere. Total disaster erupted. The very people impacted by this disaster continued to act as though everything was still okay, and I woke up.

On 2/2/2016

I was asleep but aware of a thought being heavily impressed on my mind. The thought was; *Firstfruits are before, not after. They are set aside with thought and care.*

On 2/10/2016

Today I got a call from a sister in Christ. She wanted me to come to North Carolina to witness her ordination. She offered to pay the round-trip flight. I was trying to figure out how I would pay for everything else. I told her I would check to see if I could get the time off work.

As I lay down for the night I said, "God, please tell me what You are going to do with me. Help me do whatever it is and please give me some good news! I need some good news, and so does everyone I know." With that, I allowed myself to go to sleep.

I woke up with the following words pressed deep within my spirit: "The good news is that I am real." The words felt like a source of power. My body and mind felt energized. Then I could see the word *Israel* in my mind (thoughts/imagination). Next I saw *God Israel*. When I began to say, *God-Isreal* out loud, I realized it sounds like "God is real."

That same afternoon I found out that all of my expenses had already been paid for the trip to North Carolina. The last thing the sister said to me was, "Get your book published and bring it with you. It is needed here." Well, all I can say about that is "God Israel" and "To God be the glory!"

God is still speaking to us today. What is He saying to you? This outline will assist you in recording a dream, vision, prophecy, or words that come into your spirit. They can be recorded in words and/or pictures. When you first wake up, try to remain still for a few minutes. Allow your mind to replay whatever the images and/or words were in your mind. Write down the words or draw the picture(s). The only one who needs to understand them at this point is you. That will help you to recall a dream or vision later when you actually have the time to write it all down. I find it helps when I pray and ask God to open my understanding as I record the message and the meaning on paper and research the relevance in the Bible. Sometimes I ask for insight from my pastor and others who have impacted my life in a way that has demonstrated they have an understanding of the Word of God.

Time (a.m/p.m.):

Date:

Day:

Character's name(s):

Relationship connection(s) (people, places, or things):

Key words, colors, numbers, or images:

Scene: The scene could be parts of one dream or a way to describe what happened in two or more dreams. During this process, you will acquire a way of recording your information in a way that works for you.

Scene 1 (feelings):

Scene 2 (feelings):

Scene 3 (feelings):

Synopsis:

Description:

Scriptures:

Prayer: Ask God for interpretation.

Main message:

Was the purpose of the communication from God directive, confirmation, informational, warning, or other?

GLOSSARY

All definitions are from Merriam Webster's Dictionary unless otherwise noted. This glossary is a short list of words and definitions often misunderstood. This is by no means a complete list.

cognizant: aware of something.

condemnation: a statement or expression of very strong and definite criticism or disapproval.

confession: a written or spoken statement in which you say you have done something wrong or committed a crime; the act of telling people something that makes you embarrassed, ashamed, etc.

confidence: a feeling or belief you can do something well or succeed at something; a feeling or belief someone or something is good or has the ability to succeed at something; the feeling of being certain something will happen or something is true.

consecrated: dedicated to a sacred purpose

control: to direct the behavior of (a person or animal); to cause (a person or animal) to do what you want; to have power over (something); to direct the actions or function of (something); to cause (something) to act or function in a certain way.

conviction: a strong belief or opinion.

covenant: a formal and serious agreement or promise law; a formal written agreement between two or more people, businesses, countries, etc.

debasing: to lower the value or reputation of someone or something; to make someone or something less respected.

deva: a member of a class of divine beings in the Vedic period; in the Hindu religion, these are benevolent, but in Zoroastrianism, they are evil; (in general use) a god (see https://www.google.com/#q=deva+meaning).

dogma: a belief or set of beliefs accepted by the members of a group without being questioned or doubted; a belief or set of beliefs taught by a religious organization.

endocrine: the endocrine system is the collection of glands that produce hormones to regulate metabolism, growth, development, tissue function, sexual function, reproduction, sleep and mood, among other things (see https://www.google.com/#q=Endocrine+system).

fear: In general, there are three types of fear—a positive reverence (see *Fear of the Lord: What Does It Mean?* by Mike Bennett), a response to danger (see Child Trauma Academy), and a spirit. "For God hath not given us the spirit of fear; but of power, and of love, and of a sound mind" (2 Timothy 1:7). (See https://www.biblegateway.com/passage/?search=2+Timothy+1%3A7&version=KJV.)

ferment: to go through a chemical change resulting in the production of alcohol. *Synonyms* include disquiet, unrest, fermentation, restiveness, restlessness, Sturm und Drang, turmoil, uneasiness, and unquietness.

homeostasis: the tendency toward a relatively stable equilibrium between interdependent elements, especially as maintained by physiological processes.

kingdom: a country whose ruler is a king or queen; the spiritual world of which God is king; one of the three main divisions into which natural objects are classified.

maleficent: working or productive of harm or evil.

mammon: material wealth or possessions, especially as something having a debasing influence. "You cannot serve God and mammon" (Matthew 6:24 RSV).

persevere: to continue doing something or trying to do something even though it is difficult.

pharmakeia: the use of medicine, drug, or spells (*Strong's Concordance*). (See http://biblehub.com/greek/5331.htm.)

practice: to do something again and again in order to become better at it.

precept: a rule that says how people should behave.

recompense: to give something such as money to someone as a reward or payment for loss or suffering.

repent: to feel or show you are sorry for something wrong you did; the desire to do what is right.

Salvation: the act of saving someone from sin or evil; the state of being saved from sin or evil.

sanctify: to make (something) holy.

screen games: any of various interactive games played using a specialized electronic gaming device, a computer or mobile device, and a television or other display screen along with a means to control graphic images, also including arcade machines or handheld toys (https://www.google.com/#q=screen+games+definition).

sin: "Whoever knows the right thing to do and fails to do it, for him it is sin" (James 4:17 ESV). (See http://www.ligonier.org/learn/devotionals/missing-mark.)

sober: not having one's mind affected by alcohol. It is important to stay *sober* if you are going to be driving a car. Synonyms include clearheaded and straight (http://www.merriam-webster.com/thesaurus/sober).

sovereignty: unlimited power over a country; a country's independent authority and the right to govern itself.

substance: a material of a particular kind.

system: something made of many interdependent or related parts; the national highway system allows travel from one end of the country to the other; the democratic system of checks and balances in government. Synonyms include complex and network (http://www.merriam-webster.com/thesaurus/system).

veneration: respect or awe inspired by the dignity, wisdom, dedication, or talent of a person.

wicked: not conforming to a high moral standard; morally unacceptable; a *wicked* urge to steal just for the sake of stealing. Synonyms include black, dark, evil, immoral, iniquitous, nefarious, rotten, sinful, unethical, unlawful, unrighteous, unsavory, vicious, vile, villainous, wicked, and wrong (http://www.merriam-webster.com/thesaurus/wicked).

wrestle: to seize and attempt to unbalance one another for the purpose of achieving physical mastery.

REFERENCES

(n.d.). Retrieved from Fasting for a Deeper Walk with God: http://www.altogetherlovely.org/downloads/17.%20FASTING.pdf

(n.d.). Retrieved from Ligonier.org: http://www.ligonier.org/learn/devotionals/missing-mark/?%20mobilezon

2015. Retrieved from *Merriam-Webster*: http://www.merriam-webster.com.

Anderson, J. R. 2014. *What Must I Do to Be Saved: A Devotional.* Ander Christian Foundation.

Beale, A. F. 2011. *The Divinity Code to Understanding Your Dreams and Visions.* Shippensburg, PA: Destiny Image.

Belk, C. M. 2012. *Heavenly Company.* New York: Guideposts.

Bible Hub. 2011. Retrieved from Bible Hub.com: http://biblehub.com/hebrew/4150.htm

Brausen, R. 2015. *Praying for Healing While Plannig a Funeral: A Miraculous Story of Hope.* Racine: BroadStreet Publishing Group, LLC.

Breathitt, B. 2012. *Gateway to the Seer Realm: Look Again to See Beyond the Natural.* Shippensburg, PA: Destiny Image Publishers, Inc.

chalden. (n.d.).

Crowl, L. A. 1995. *The Seven-Day Week and the Meanings of the Names of the Days.* Retrieved from www.crowl.org: http://www.crowl.org/lawrence/time/days.html

DeBruyn, P. L. 2007. *Opening the Third Eye Christians Beware.* Retrieved from kimolsen.wordpress.com: https://kimolsen.wordpress.com/2007/08/31/opening-the-third-eye-christians-beware/

Durgs are Sorcery. (n.d.). Retrieved from letusreason.org: http://www.letusreason.org/Curren10.htm

Ferrell, D. A. 2011. *Pharmakeia; A Hidden Assassin.* Ponte Vedra: Ana Mendez Ferrell Inc.

Gerasimo, P. 2015. *Emotional Biochemistry: Experience Life.* Retrieved from experiencelive.com: https://experiencelife.com/article/emotional-biochemistry/

Hamon, J. 2000, 2016. *Dreams and Visions; Understanding and Interpreting God's Messsages to You.* Ada, MI: Chosen Books.

homeostasis. (n.d.). Retrieved from thesaurus.com: http://www.thesaurus.com/browse/homeostasis

How Wounds Heal. (n.d.). Retrieved from http://www.hopkinsmedicine.org/: http://www.hopkinsmedicine.org/healthlibrary/conditions/surgical_care/how_wounds_heal_134,143/

Institute in Basic Live Principles. (n.d.). Retrieved from iblp.org: http://iblp.org/questions/how-does-god-speak

Jackson, P., director. 2013. *The Hobbit: The Desolation of Smaug* (Motion Picture).

maleficent. (n.d.). Retrieved from dictionary.reference.com: http://dictionary.reference.com/browse/maleficent

McMillan, B. 2009. *Illustrated Atlas of the Human Body.* McMahons Point: Weldon Owen Pty, Ltd.

Milligan, I. 1997. *Understanding the Dreams You Dream; Biblical Keys for Hearing God's Voice in the Night.* Shippensburg, PA: Treasure House.

Muehlenberg, B. (n.d.). *Fellowship of the Burning Heart.* Retrieved from billmuehlenbert.com: http://billmuehlenberg.com/2011/08/28/the-fellowship-of-the-burning-heart/

Munroe, M. 2011. *Understanding Your Original Place in God's Kingdom: Your Original Purpose for Existence.* Shippensburg, PA: Destiny Image.

occult. (n.d.). Retrieved from wordcentral.com: http://wordcentral.com/cgi-bin/thesaurus?book=Thesaurus&va=occult

Oppenheimer, M. 2014. *Drugs Sre Sorcery.* Retrieved from Welcome to Let Us Reason Ministries: http://www.letusreason.org/Curren10.htm

PhD, C. L. 2009. *Who Switched Off My Brain? Revised: Controlling Toxic Thoughts and Emotions.* Southlake, TX: Inprov, Ltd.

Phillips, P. 1990. *Turmoil In THe Toybox.* Starburst.

Ramirez, J. 2012. *Out of the Devil's Cauldron: A Journey from Darkness to Light.* New York: Heaven & Earth Media.

Repentance. (n.d.). Retrieved from en.wikipedia.org: https://en.wikipedia.org/wiki/Repentance

Roberts, D. R. (n.d.). *Pharmakeia: The Sorcerer's Wand.* Retrieved from Pharmakeia: The Sorcerer's Wand: www.youtube.com/watch?v=5gDnDE_WpU8

Sabbath–Presents of God Ministries. (n.d.). Retrieved from http://www.remnantofgod.org/sabbath.htm

Scott, R., director. 2014. *Exodus: Gods & Kings* [Motion Picture].

spell. (n.d.). Retrieved from thefreedictionary.com: http://www.thefreedictionary.com/spell

The Heart Has a "Brain" in Consciousness: Intuition and Mindful Living. (n.d.). Retrieved from Mindful Muscel; Mindfulness Changes Everything: http://www.mindfulmuscle.com/heart-has-consciousness-knows-before-brain/

Were did the names of the week come from? (n.d.). Retrieved from www.almanac.com: http://www.almanac.com/fact/where-did-the-names-of-the-days

What does it mean to have a seared conscience? (n.d.). Retrieved from gotquestions.org: http://www.gotquestions.org/seared-conscience.html

What is yoga? (n.d.). Retrieved from cai.org: https://www.cai.org/testimonies/spiritual-deception-yoga and http://www.thefreedictionary.com/Pata%C3%B1jali

Definitions from 222.merriam-webster.com unless otherwise noted

Deliverance: https://gotquestions.org/deliverance.html
Discernment: http://biblehub.com/topical/dbt/8227.htm
Dreams: https://en.oxforddictionaries.com/definition/us/dream
Faith: http://pediaa.com/difference-between-faith-and-belief
Fasting: my definition.
Fellowship: http://www.whatchristianswanttoknow.com/christian-fellowshi-quotes-22-edifying-quotes
Holy Days: http://www.triumphpro.com/holy-days-book.pdf
Prayer: http://www.tellingthetruth.org/hot-topics/prayer/what-is-prayer.aspx
Repentance: http://www.encyclopedia.com/humanities/dictionaries-thesauruses-pictures-and-press-releases/repent
Vision: https://en.oxforddictionaries.com/definition/vision
Adultery: http://www.merriam-webster.com/dictionary/adultery

Charm: http://www.merriam-webster.com/dictionary/charm

Charmer: http://www.merriam-webster.com/thesaurus/charmer

Chaldean: https://www.google.com/#q=A+member+of+an+ancient+semitic+people+that+became+dominant+in+Babylonia%3B+a+person+versed+in+the+occult+arts

Days of the week names: http://www.livescience.com/45432-days-of-the-week.html

Divination: http://www.merriam-webster.com/dictionary/divination

Entertainment: http://www.merriam-webster.com/dictionary/enchanter

Familiar spirit: https://gotquestions.org/familiar-spirits.html

Familial: http://www.merriam-webster.com/dictionary/familial

Graven image: http://www.gotquestions.org/graven-image.html,

Holidays tradition: http://www.nazarite.net/evil-holidays.html

Horoscope: http://www.merriam-webster.com/dictionary/horoscope

Idolatry: http://www.merriam-webster.com/dictionary/idolatry

Magic: http://www.merriam-webster.com/dictionary/magic

Necromancy: http://www.merriam-webster.com/dictionary/necromancy

Scrying: https://en.oxforddictionaries.com/definition/us/scry

Seared consciences: http://www.kingdomcitizens.org/one-womans-perspective/beware-of-a-seared-conscience

Spell: http://www.merriam-webster.com/thesaurus/spell

Spiritualism: https://www.google.com/#q=spiritualism+definition

Superstition: http://www.merriam-webster.com/dictionary/superstition

Warlock: http://www.merriam-webster.com/dictionary/warlock

Witch: http://www.merriam-webster.com/dictionary/witch

Witchcraft: http://www.merriam-webster.com/dictionary/witchcraft

Wizard: http://www.merriam-webster.com/dictionary/wizard

Yoga: https://ahdictionary.com/word/search.html?q=yogic

Deva: https://www.google.com/#q=deva+meaning

Endocrine: https://www.google.com/#q=Endocrine+system

Pharmakeia: http://biblehub.com/greek/5331.htm

Screen games: https://www.google.com/#q=screen+games+definition

Sin: http://www.ligonier.org/learn/devotionals/missing-mark

Sober: http://www.merriam-webster.com/thesaurus/sober

System: http://www.merriam-webster.com/thesaurus/system

Wicked: http://www.merriam-webster.com/thesaurus/wicked

Transgress: https://books.google.com/books?id=DLt_CwAAQBAJ&pg=PA25&lpg=PA25&dq=To+violate+a+command+or+law:+to+go+beyond+a+boundary+or+limit+of+what+God+says+to+do+or+not+to+do&source=bl&ots=_yo1FBKepM&sig=RfWA27g_BPJ6Cs NqUsUkNlED3Fs&hl=en&sa=X&ved=0ahUKEwiFgvHFluPPAhWr7YMKHRiWBB4Q6AEIHDAA#v=onepage&q=To%20violate%20a%20command%20or%20law%3A%20to%20go%20beyond%20a%20boundary%20or%20limit%20of%20what%20God%20says%20to%20do%20or%20not%20to%20do&f=false

Iniquity: http://www.gotquestions.org/iniquity-sin-transgression.html

ABOUT THE AUTHOR

Paris Moore, a native of St. Paul, Minnesota, now lives in Plymouth, Minnesota. She has been married to Larry Moore for thirty-two years. They have been blessed with two children, a son-in-law, a daughter-in-law, and two grandchildren.

Moore invited Jesus Christ into her heart more than thirty years ago. While in prayer, she asked God to lead her to a church that would teach her how to hear from Him the first time all the time. She also asked God to guide her to a place where she could learn how to study the Bible, activate the information she gathered, and apply it to her life. That's when God led her to the Moving On Up Church in Minneapolis, Minnesota, where she earned her minister's license in 1988.

During those years, under the leadership of Dr. Jill and Apostle William Jackson, Moore was given the opportunity to practice what she learned.

Over the years she shared her insights on prayer and leadership while leading Bible studies and managing the hospitality committee and other church events. She ministered through hospital visits, funeral support, prison ministry, and intercessory prayer, and she preached the Word of God to the congregation. She also exalted God through her mime ministry.

Her passion for youth led her to create and facilitate a Bible-based science and engineering summer program for youth.

In 2012, Minister Moore researched, developed, and co-presented "Video Games through the Eyes of Children" at a School Age Care Conference in St. Paul. Being a researcher at heart, she was curious to know how children and youth in general defined violence, so she began to ask questions. It became increasingly clear even though she and the children were looking at the same images on the same screen at the same time, their perceptions were completely different. In these conversations she became the student, and the children the teachers.

Although the presentation was for the secular community, God was teaching her what happened when anyone interacted with a demonic system of delivery. The following were core takeaways from this research:

- Many children are losing the ability to express what they are feeling, seeing, or experiencing during real events. Instead they *are* applying video game language to real events. Moore calls this communication "video game real-time language."
- Meaningful, intergenerational conversations seem to be on the decline.
- We *don't* want to stop children from being who they are. We *do want* to protect them from deceptive and invisible plots by the adversary as they grow away from the world.

Moore was surprised to find just how relevant this information was to our spiritual walk with Christ.

Moore is now responding to the call of God, which came during her prayer time. These are the words that came to her spirit. "I am giving you a heavy mantle to tell people to seek Me while I may be found. Don't worry about where to start. Just start *somewhere*. Tell them I love them. I made them for My glory to walk and fellowship with Me. They are the delight of My heart when they praise Me, when they give to others, and when they help one another in My name. Come to Me all those who are heavy-laden, and I will give you rest."

This is my *somewhere*, and you are the people. I pray you are blessed and strengthened as you study the Bible, committing to a deeper walk with God. You are needed on the front lines of faith.

Printed in the United States
By Bookmasters